TONESMITH

I0388600

ALSO BY AL BASILE

A Lit House – 100 poems 1975-2011

Cds

Down on Providence Plantation
Shaking the Soul Tree
Red Breath
Blue Ink
Groovin' in the Mood Room
The Tinge
Soul Blue 7
At Home Next Door
The Goods
Woke Up in Memphis
Swing n' Strings
B's Expression
Mid-Century Modern
Quiet Money

The author's reading of the poems in this book
may be accessed at:
http://albasile.com/Tonesmith_-_audio_files.html

TONESMITH

One Hundred Poems, 2012–2016

Al Basile

Antrim House
Simsbury, Connecticut

Copyright © 2017 by Alfred C. Basile

Except for short selections reprinted for purposes of
book review, all reproduction rights are reserved.
Requests for permission to replicate should
be addressed to the publisher.

Library of Congress Control Number: 2017939470

ISBN: 978-1-943826-30-8

First Edition, 2017

Printed & bound by Ingram Spark

Book design by Rennie McQuilkin

Front cover artwork ("Elijah's Friends")
by Stephanie Gehring

Author photograph by Meghan Sepe

Antrim House
860.217.0023
AntrimHouse@comcast.net
www.AntrimHouseBooks.com
21 Goodrich Road, Simsbury, CT 06070

To those unknown poets whose work, which would have nourished the lives of those it touched, has been lost, suppressed, or forgotten, and is destined to remain undiscovered.

ACKNOWLEDGMENTS

Grateful acknowledgment to the editors of the following publications, in which these poems first appeared, some in earlier versions:

Brilliant Corners: "Waiting for Ellington"
The Dark Horse: "Black and Tan Fantasy"
First Things: "The Coventry Carol"
Italian Americana: "Geode"
Literary Imagination: "War Games, 1953"
Literary Matters: "A Straw in the Wind" (co-winner
   of the 2015 Meringoff Award for Poetry)
Louisiana Literature: "Morning Glory"
The New Criterion: "Sgt. Darden"
Raintown Review: "Demand, Then Supply"

Thanks to Christopher Ricks for his warm and illuminating response upon being the first to hear many of the poems in this volume, often within days of their creation.

INTRODUCTION

OR, GLADLY

When the thought of a poem – the thought that will in due course become a poem – comes to Al Basile's mind (and not only mind, since heart and lungs, mouth and ears, are all to be gratefully respected), his response to the dear whisper – *How about a poem?* – will characteristically be "Gladly". Gladly, as courteously gratified to receive and to accept the invitation; gladly, as how the poem will find itself created, performed, conducted, and will conduct itself. With gladness.

The same, then, goes for an invitation from the poet/singer/songwriter/horn-player. . . : *How about some thoughts about these poems?*

Gladly. Of course.

Any such thoughts, though, must take care not to assume the air – or the airs – of a review, even while holding the poems firmly, attentively, in view and in re-view. Seeking what the great poet-critic William Empson called "the right handle to take hold of the bundle", I decided to take up the line of English poetry that best apprehends the power of *gladly*: "And gladly would he learn, and gladly teach". For Geoffrey Chaucer's Clerk of Oxenford, learning and teaching were in perfect balance and harmony, gladly enjoying that one sweet word, not at all afraid of saying something again, in the confidence that not being fearful of repetition – yes, embracing it – is essential to both learning and teaching. As it plainly is to song and to poetry. Of the essence.

Tonesmith has at its heart the enduring reciprocity of learning and teaching. At its heart, not only as at once stability and movement ("That made my heart too small to hold its blood", as Keats felt it, or "Felt in the blood and felt along the heart", for Wordsworth), but in the simplest and most straightforward sense. The hundred poems appear alphabetically by title (and learning the alphabet, like teaching it, was always one of the happiest of feats), from "A Burl for the Carving" through to "Winter Light". Midway, at the center

~*vii*~

of it all, there is a sequence of poems that constitutes something better than a run of them: "How I Learned About Aging", "How I Learned about Leadership", "How I Learned About Omertá", "How I Learned About Self-Determination", "How I Learned About Signs From Above", and "How I Learned About Solitude", this last one recalling his very young self (three!) and his mother's leaving the house though not for long:

> I see my mother walk across the street
>
> below me. Then she disappears. I know
>
> there is a corner store two blocks away.
>
> First time now I feel that I'm alone.
>
> First time now, I feel that she'll be back.

Take the full force of the exactitude that chose to follow the latter, though not the former, "now" with a comma. Time must have a stop; trust must have a comma.

You soon become signally aware of what this poet is not only up for, and up to, but up against: all those considerations and factors which make both teaching and learning so much more vulnerable, imperiled, than we would wish to hope. So I want to – even feel the need to – sketch the imaginative resources with which Al Basile holds off the dangers that cannot but prowl around his accessible domain. The danger, for instance, of sounding *school-masterly* ("And God the Father turns a School-Divine", even in *Paradise Lost*, or so Alexander Pope judged). Or, God save the mark, *professorial.* Or *didactic*, that very classroom word. Or, oh, *indoctrination.* Or the propensity of the beautiful word "learn" to turn into its ugly sibling. Blessedly, the appeal in these poems ("The lesson learned / remains") is crucially different from the cruel self-righteousness of *That'll larn ya*, or even of *That'll teach you a lesson.* Here the matter is quite other, lucidly different ("now that the truth about it's out"):

> So learn the lesson you've been shown –
>
> try leaving well enough alone.
>
> ("Disturbing the Peace")

But such will continue to be, necessarily, the warnings, threats, animadversions, insinuations, that are likely to be bent these days upon any poem that takes it upon itself to &c.

With then, above it all, up there, the lofty accusation of *naivety*, of apparently believing, as people so oddly used to do, that the arts, and especially literature, have as one of their high demands, aspirations, and achievements, the realization of and the imparting of *wisdom,* that markedly old-fashioned – let's face it, obsolete – property.

Wisdom, in these poems, though, is not allowed to appear as is-suing from a wise-acre, or as going in for wisecracks, or as telling oneself or anyone else to wise up, or (at the pompous opposite end) thinking of Wisdom as forever rearing its Seven Pillars. None of that; in these humane poems, wisdom is the commonalty of experience, shared by the living with the dead: the past, "insisting it exists". This is something that the poems themselves find the right terms for, among them the good old words themselves. *Wise*, as in "The Man Who Couldn't Afford to Buy a Vowel":

> Though he can walk and run, he doesn't dance.
>
> He can read a book, but not the papers.
>
> He can know it all, yet not be wise.

And *wisdom*, as in "Mushroom Hunters, 1957":

> and though I was a child and uninvited
>
> I wondered how the wisdom carried over
>
> that led them to the aspens, oaks, or birches
>
> which sheltered, huddled at their bases, all
>
> the rich array of fungi that they prized.

"A nest, a toad, a fungus, or a flower": Pope, himself "The man for wisdom's various arts renown'd". *Wisdom*!

Critical prejudices – "current wisdom" – and any low companions of such prejudices are not skirted by the poems but are even prized by them; faced, head on, and laughingly frowned down.

How? Foremost and first, by having a sense of true humor. Particularly, as to when this had better be rueful humor. Take the honorable acknowledgment of how easily a tone (*the* tone) may be in danger of slipping: "No point in putting it to them like that". Or the danger of an anecdote's turning gnarled and folksy – and the honorable eluding of this:

> I never got to say what I had learned –
>
> secrets which I had no right to know
>
> and couldn't have explained.
>
> ("He Learns a Lesson from a Star-Crossed Letter")

Or a well-turned admonition's being in danger of turning sententious – but fortunately open to being redeemed by the true voice of conversational verse: "The thing is, never give them what they want". Or the reminder that, among the many things that proverbs may teach us, is their willingness to be, on occasion, contested: "when both are good, two cooks are not too many".

The poet as teacher and learner, then, is not pretending otherwise, and he has humor to hand. All this is not a matter of being *in the teaching business* since it isn't or shouldn't be a business, though this poet is rightly proud of his decades of service to the teaching profession. (And of his detestation of "The Gradegrubbers".) Openness is all, as not only in "How I Learned . . . " but as in the many other poems that ensure that the particular "How I. . . " sequence doesn't enjoy a monopoly: poems such as "A Teaching Moment: Brown University, 1971" (where a teaching moment is understood to amount to so much less than a teaching momentum), or "Learning the Wall", or "Learning to Hear", acute in comprehending, with the utmost patience of a classroom, the difference between those equally but differently valuable things, learning to listen and learning to hear. Or there is the difference between teaching and *training*: military in "Sgt. Darden"; vocal, "legitimately trained, a little thin", in "The Coventry Carol"; punitive, in "Dark Certainties":

~*x*~

But he will not be comforted. He takes

the taste of iron in his mouth for justice.

Whoever taught him punishment has trained

him to continue it now they are gone.

"Tonesmith" – the poem that gives the volume its title but is rightly not granted pride of place either at the opening or at the closing of the volume, simply taking instead its due place within the alphabetical sequence – does itself open with a reminder of a solid fact.

Like any other score, these words are merely

shadows on the page, a rough instruction

to the reader, two dimensional:

until you hear me speak, them, incomplete.

Do not, gentle reader, believe him. Do, though, winnow his words. The comic spirit that chose to complete those lines with the word *incomplete* ought to put us on our guard, as ought the bantering mock-modesty of *merely*, the ingratiating shrug of "a rough instruction", and much else. But we know what Al Basile means, and we should do so even if the physical reality were not just of two dimensions but of two media: book and recording of the poet. There are to be readers and listeners; the artist will gladly allow us an audience with him, and we shall be his audience, gladly.

Needless to say, I want to say that for me the words on the page are unlike a score, as well as like one; and that the words on the page are not incomplete until uttered by the poet; rather, they have a different completion on the page from that which they enjoy when in the air, from his cords and chords. But then I know I need to watch my tongue, and must not speak of the book *Tonesmith* as coming with a recording, lest the recording sing out (excuse *me*) that it is the other way round: the recording comes with a book.

As to teaching and "a rough instruction", the classic statement (as so often) is by T.S. Eliot. On his recording of *Four Quartets* in 1947:

A recording of a poem read by its author is no more definitive an "interpretation" than a recording of a symphony conducted by the composer. The poem, if it is of any depth and complexity, will have meanings in it concealed from the author, and should be capable of being read in many ways, and with a variety of emotional emphases.

A good poem, indeed, is one which even the most accomplished reading cannot exhaust.

What the recording of a poem by its author can and should preserve, is the way that poem sounded to the author when he had finished it. . .

Another reader, reciting the poem, need not feel bound to reproduce these rhythms; but, if he has studied the author's version, he can assure himself that he is departing from it deliberately, and not from ignorance.

But then Mr. Eliot, though a poet indeed, was not singer/songwriter/horn-player. . . So let the more-than-author of the multimediated *Tonesmith* have the last words:

Heard face to face, they add what else a word

can do in company: tell you a story,

paint a picture, raise the dead, and tell

that truth that makes you laugh or starts you thinking.

You'll get that from the page. But hear me play

these compositions on my instrument.

Christopher Ricks

TABLE OF CONTENTS

3   A Burl for the Carving

4   A Cardinal in March

5   A Liver Sausage Dinner

8   A Minute's Choice

10   A Pang of Sparrows

11   A Roman Idyll

13   A Sidewalk Tree

14   A Stolen Gift

18   A Straw in the Wind

20   A Teaching Moment

22   A Whitman Update

23   An Audience of One

24   "As a Man Is, So He Sees"

25   At the Beach

26   Black and Tan Fantasy

28   Black Pearls, 1942

30   Bossa Antigua

31   Cans on the Shelf

32   Christmas Morning in Rumford, 2012

33   Counting Without Numbers

34   Dark Certainties

36   Demand, Then Supply

37   Diagnostic

39   Disturbing the Peace

40   Dotting the Eye

42   Flaming Youth

43   For S.S.

44   Geode

45   Grand Canal, August 1972

46   He Is as the Wind

47   He Learns a Lesson From a Star-Crossed Letter

~xiii~

49   His Daemon Tells It Like It Is

50   Hope Speaks

52   How I Learned About Aging

53   How I Learned About Leadership

54   How I Learned About Omertá

56   How I Learned About Self-Determination

58   How I Learned About Signs From Above

59   How I Learned About Solitude

60   I Play Roy Eldridge's Trumpet

62   In Praise of Weakness

63   In Single File

64   Indolence

65   It Was Different in the Fifties

66   Johnny Hodges and Cleopatra

67   JR Declines a Camping Invitation

68   Learning the Wall

69   Learning to Hear

71   "Lest You Dash Thy Foot Against a Stone"

73   Licking the Beater

74   Locks and Doors

76   Maya's First Hard Boiled Egg

78   Misdirection of the Natural World

79   Mistaken Notions of the Dead

81   Morning Glory

83   Mushroom Hunters, 1957

85   My Bow Ties

87   Nightlight

88   Not Lost, Found

91   Not the Thing Itself

92   1+1=One

93   One Saved From the Flame

94   Other Waters

96   Outliers

98   Patching a Flat

100   Piu Forte

102   Punch Drunk

~xiv~

104 Rainstick
105 Roy's Unlearned Lesson
106 Secret Bird
107 Sense and Sound
108 Sensible Doubt
109 Seven Hundredths of an Ounce
110 Sgt. Darden
112 Song Unsung
113 Stazione Termini, Rome 1972
114 Stone Love
115 Straight Outta Antiquity
116 Tempo Rubato
117 The Coventry Carol
118 The Cracked Plate
119 The Ghost of Easters Past
121 The Gradegrubbers
122 The Horn and Me
124 The Man Who Couldn't Afford to Buy a Vowel
125 The Passing of the Age of Giants
127 The Poisoned Pawn
128 The Prisoner's Confession to the Jailer
130 The Tree of Secrets
131 The Winnowing
136 To My Brother the Dancer
137 Tonesmith
138 Two Simple Verses on the Way Things Are
139 Waiting for Ellington
140 Waldszenen
141 War Games, 1953
142 Well-lit Corridors
143 Windows and Doors
144 Winter Light

146 About the Author
147 About the Book

The heart of the melody can never be put down on paper.
Pablo Casals

TONESMITH

A Burl for the Carving

"Human life is conditioned and unfree."
  — I Ching

Hammer at the matter how you will;
close-grained as it is, its knots and burrs,
concealed until the first assay, deflect
and redirect the chisel's edge, admit
no easy progress, and assure an outcome
imprecise, wrought fine by will but blunted
where permission from the language is denied.

A Cardinal in March

Returning home on foot early one morning
heartsore at twenty, brooding and rebuffed,
I paused beside a maple, summery,
thick with green and warbling the trill
of some contented thrush, only to note
I couldn't tell where it had been concealed
until it flew away. The metaphor's appeal
was strong, the poem it evoked ironic,
stewing in its youthful juices.

                                    Now
much later in the day for metaphor,
what penetrates my kitchen window panes,
shut tight against the cold, once more is birdsong,
precise and clear, its company a sight
of scarlet perched on sketched-in winter branch.
The shrubbery has withered into something
like truth. The cardinal makes no show of hiding.
Its glissing *whoot-to-woo* and monotone
wheet greets me: *wheet wheet wheet wheet wheet wheet wheet.*

A Liver Sausage Dinner

One day on Atwells Avenue I passed
a butcher's shop. The Hill was still Italian
then, a neighborhood that mostly served
its own. Now it's gone International.

A hand-drawn window sign said "Liver Sausage,"
and I remembered once my father said
he'd loved them as a kid, but hadn't had
or even seen one, in he couldn't say
how long. They mixed in bits of orange peel,
he said – that cut the liver taste. His mouth
would water at the thought of them; but now
nobody seemed to sell them any more.

I bought a package. This was on a Friday;
next day I would be driving north to visit.
It's more than twenty years ago – my folks
had moved into a little house when Dad
retired, and the kitchen didn't give
my Mom much room to operate. That was
to figure in to what would happen next.

On Saturday I made the ninety miles
in good time, getting in just after two.
My Dad was sitting at the table reading;
I swung the brown bag up and put it down
in front of him. "I brought you a surprise."

"What's that?" he said, without glancing up from
his article. "Just take a look," I said.

~5~

His first reaction was astonishment,
which broadened shortly to a grin. "It's liver
sausage. Where'd you get this?"

"Fed'ral Hill."

"We've got to try this. Gracie, can you make
these for dinner?" Yes, she could: my Mom
loved rising to a culinary challenge.

The balance of the afternoon was ripe
with expectation. When at five my Mom
got out a roasting pan, my hawk-eyed Dad
barked "What's that for?" – suspicion in his tone,
for he was on familiar terms with pans
and burners, having been an Army cook
in the Pacific during World War Two.
He'd cooked for hundreds at a time, and made
do with powdered eggs and bartered produce.
"I'll brown them in the oven with potatoes
and cut up peppers," Mom reported calmly;
till now her mastery had been unquestioned.

"That's not the way you make a liver sausage,"
my Dad said evenly, his patience for
the uninitiated audible.

"Oh yeah?" my Mom said, rising to the bait,
"And how is that?"

"You fry them in a skillet
with some onions," Dad replied.

No act
partook more of the sacred in our house

~6~

than choosing, handling, and preparing food:
each daily meal was Biblical. I sensed
a sudden rise of storm clouds, and assumed
my customary role: to keep the peace.
Stretching out my arms, palms down (*"Hear me,
O Israel..."*), a homespun Solomon,
I uttered a decree. "We will divide
the sausages; *you* make them one way, *you*
the other, and we'll all judge the results."

It was a kind of dance that they engaged in
then, around the counters and the stove,
inhabiting the modest space at turns, without
obstruction or dispute, as though Astaire
and Rogers, moving to a music they alone
could hear, each traded off the lead. When done
at last, the difference from dance was dinner.

The liver sausage satisfied both ways
and soon was gone, while they kept on display
the mystery of an enduring marriage:
when both are good, two cooks are not too many.

~7~

A Minute's Choice

Back from the Rock one August afternoon,
driving the straightaway down Hope, I see
a black pillar of smoke that marks my block
as though to show me my way home. Before
I can get close, the Hook and Ladders force me
to park three streets away, and I approach
on foot the squad of firemen swarming by
the cordon of equipment. Bolts of water
arc up into a shock of flame that points
skyward for thirty feet, at least, above
the blunt shell of the building next to mine
but my apartment house, still white, appears
untouched across a narrow alleyway behind,
between both structures, as the empty roar
of fire and hiss of disappearing water
add instead of cancel in the din,
and any small and subtle shift of wind
will send up my belongings, sacrifice
demanded by this sudden, angry god
that's brought its elemental show of force
into my neighborhood. I stride up to
the entryway; a figure, helmeted
and clad in canvas, rubber, metal-clasped,
stands in my way. "You can't go in," he says,
"It could go up at any time." I stare
beyond his shoulders at the door. "But all
I have is in there – everything –" I hear,
and I must be the one who said it, though
I don't see how; I only see the door.

He takes a beat and eyes me evenly.
"One minute," he replies, and steps aside.

The bounding up the stairs is just a blur.
Once past the lock I stalk straight to the back.
The bedroom window's open to the flame,
and if my building doesn't catch, the smoke
will still wreak havoc. Both my palms come down
against the frame and push it to the sill.
The dancing light cools down behind the pane.
I turn, and purpose guides my steps; I pause,
pick up my trumpet case in my left hand,
catch up my novel manuscripts one two
from where they sit and grip them in my right.
No pause then to the door and out. Within
the minute given I'm back on the street.

I lock two-fisted treasure in my car,
retrace my steps, drawn back to face the flame,
questioning the wind, helpless to fate.
The conflagration, fed by a gas line,
does not submit until the underground
network of pipes is reached and strangled shut,
and then the flames subside. Next door is left
a husk, but all throughout an hour the wind
has held direction, and my building's safe.

Two hands to test a life. How did I know
what must be saved? When cut back to a moment,
choice was simple: Yet-To-Be-Created,
and Irreplaceable. The necessary.
The horn to finish practice for the day;
the books, my only copies, slow accretions
of a thousand days that will not be repeated.
With these demands my hands are full. The past
and present, carried forward for the future.

A Pang of Sparrows

As though emotion grew, less like the tulip,
a solo bloom emerging from a stem,
more like an influence of elements,
each one too subtle to assert itself
alone, but swelled in concert to a cry
(some unseen agent tipping the cascade
that makes the many seem a single form),
a murmuring of signals out along
their phone line perch releases in a rush
a pang of sparrows, leaping in the near
and tilting off into the middle distance.

A Roman Idyll

Two Welsh nurses on vacation, one
native Roman boyfriend-guide, and I
went out to EUR, south of the city
one night in August forty years ago.
What passed for an amusement park was mostly
row on row of shooting galleries.
The crackling uproar of the pellet rifles
cut ribbons through the hubbub of the crowd.
We picked a random booth, manned by a short
mustachioed proprietor whose eyes
glistened at the chance to goad a showoff.
The nurses needed to be entertained.

Sharp colors clustered on the side walls, prizes
tacked up to distract the eye as ducks
swam grinning left to right and upside down.
"What's the biggest prize?" I asked. A smile
jumped up into the owner's face: he pointed.
On a shelf, amid blue bears and yellow
rabbits, floppy-eared and kiddy-cuddly,
one fat bottle of spumante wine
to satisfy discerning adult tastes.

"What do I have to do?" I asked. A narrow
strip of paper hung down from the ceiling
gleaming white, five inches wide. The man
pointed down at a BB rifle. "Cut
the paper. Twenty-five shots in a clip,"
he said, as our interpreter reported.

I paid my *lire* as I made my plan.
The BB holes were small, the paper firm

~*11*~

and wide, comparatively. Nibbling bit
by bit from left to right might not succeed
before I counted one to twenty-five.

The rifle was laughably light. I picked
it up and steadied it, my elbow tight
into my side, breathed halfway out, and sighted.
I put nine shots, a line of periods
to punctuate the paper, equal widths
apart. Then one shot in each space between.
The paper, severed, fell at seventeen.

A Sidewalk Tree

This sycamore, that can't conceal its growth
in deeper, wider wrinkles like its neighbor
oaks and maples, has no act to drop,
no snake-like wholesale shedding of a skin
that smacks of re-invention; it instead
(as though relaxing from a kept-up guard
in halting manner, at a glacial pace)
comes clean of pieces jigsawed from its puzzle,
uninterlocked in layers mottling down
from browns through greens to fresh tans smooth
and gleaming on its pale unblemished surface,
except where some sharp point, directed by
a halting hand, has scored *ALWAYS ALONE.*

A Stolen Gift

(long shot)

It's summer, Sixty-Two. Five teens emerge
from blue-green pines and hemlocks, single file
along a narrow path down past the edge
of water in a flat New Hampshire lake.
They carry household items in their hands
like prizes, heads down, walking silently
as though not in a hurry. Then the line
distends; the last two lag behind, a boy
and girl in conversation, hesitant.
The girl is younger than the boy, and taller.
She stops and sways a little by the lake,
an object in each hand of equal size
and shape. The boy, intent, insistent, speaks.
She listens as the others disappear.
There is a breeze; bright water laps the shore
and sparkles its disturbance. With her left
she reaches out to him an offering.
He takes it solemnly; she turns and throws
what's in her right hand curving in an arc
high in the air and far. It flashes as
the sunlight catches it, and then, as though
on film in slowing motion, it descends
into the water clear on clear, like white
of snowflake into white of snow. Subdued,
the two walk on in silence once again.

~14~

(closeup)

A clear glass candlestick, hexagonal
and cleanly cut at base and top, its stem
six sided too but softened on the edges,
swelling in a gentle curve along
its middle. Through four decades I could never
bring myself to part with it. Intrinsic
value didn't count in the equation:
it couldn't have been much, especially
without its matching partner. What it meant
was worth more, complicated by its past.

(two-shots)

Back when the world was black and white, and wrong
and right were warring kingdoms, I relied
on loyalties I'd learned by rote. Reduced
to a duality, the choice of yes
or no was simplified. And so I knew
that it was wrong when kids from down around
the lake shore road said "There's a house back in
the woods that's closed up for the summer – let's
go out there and break in." I would have said
no, but I was fourteen, and I had
a girlfriend for the first time, and we liked
each other so much we did everything
together, and she had an older sister
who ran with a fast crowd and never asked
her to come along, except this once –

As soon as we had left the gravel road
and disappeared into the trees, thinned out
into a line, our footfalls soft against

the yielding bed of brown pine needles, I
began to pick at them. Predictions dire
as I could muster flew; their consciences,
stolid as scraps of clay, refused to quicken.
Not until we reached the house, brown-shingled,
alone there in the woods, with shades undrawn,
did words begin to strike. A window, wedged
and leveraged open, led to the unlocking;
we entered at the door like any guests
while I kept up my warnings. We were teens:
they barely seemed to pay attention, yet
the moments crackled as they passed; expecting
some sudden shift, excitable, our eyes
like grasshoppers leapt up and settled on
first this, then that – lampshades, low wicker chairs,
the ormolu clock speaking from the mantle
that we were stealing time itself from someone.
So when I pegged two corner floodlights, perched
on a gunmetal box with dials and switches –
light in an emergency, it seemed –
as a new anti-theft surveillance system
complete with distant warning signaling,
their mood broke like a fever. In a panic
they each grabbed something for their trouble, and
shot out the door like groceries spilled from
a too-filled paper bag, wet at the bottom.

We scuttled back along our trail as though
pursued, and when we reached the road I caught
my breath, and saw that she had taken them,
the candlesticks, from off the mantle. While
the others hurried on ahead, we lingered
by the lake. I pleaded with her not
to keep what she had stolen, but we had

~16~

no thought of going back. She bowed her head
and couldn't look at me, but offered one
of that matched set of two. I didn't know
why it seemed right to take it; when she turned
and threw the other out into the lake
(we knew the water there was deepest), I
could see I'd made her do it, yet I didn't
follow suit. And she accepted that.
We walked back then without a word, and never
brought it up again thereafter. One
glass candlestick of two, it stood alone
for decades after on apartment shelves,
its secret kept. Dizzy Gillespie, asked
once about his influences, and if
he thought that taking from the older players
before him was a kind of theft, said "No,
that's a gift – and you can't steal a gift."

(iris)

The girl, the romance, and the candlestick
have vanished from my life. The lesson learned
remains: What lies beyond the differences
between the rights and wrongs we can discern
is harder to see – hard as seeing clear
glass settled in clear water, when a breeze
disturbs our sight, out where the lake is deepest.

A Straw in the Wind

When they reach the river they all find
a clearing where the current seems to slow,
but heavy lying mists obscure their sight.
No judging distance to the farther bank,
and anyone who steps into the flow
immediately disappears, enveloped.

These souls submit to many difficulties.
They find themselves in such a weakened state
that progress is well-nigh impossible.
Their reason is confounded; they can make
no sense of what their eyes and ears reveal.
At first their limbs cannot obey their will;
their tongues are loose and inarticulate,
and as they make their way they presently
forget the feel of solid ground, the clear-
eyed sight of that bright world where everything
appears exactly as it is, the rest
untroubled of the still place they have left.

How terrifying it must be, to labor
uncertainly in swift and plunging currents
ceaseless except for change, often deceived
by shapes that loom nearby and disappear
again into the dim, unsettling mist.
Not one can see the hand before his face,
or guess how far to reach the other side,
though they tell many stories of that place
to urge each other on. No one recalls
his former state; confusion rules, and keeps

each separated from his neighbor, though
they often drift into another's path,
supposing greater distances from some
nearby, and close proximities to others
far away. Collisions can't be helped
but few can see them for the comedies
they are. Though limited by ignorance,
most are deadly serious about themselves.

Their greatest fear is to be swept away
and lost forever in the surging waters,
shrouded in mist, never to know a clear
moment of peace and the relief of landfall.
Some hesitate before they step into
that current, draw back from its scudding edge,
troubled by the unfamiliar, sensing
consequences, holding for the most
propitious moment, pausing at the thought
of all they must abandon to begin
the solitary trial they call life.

A Teaching Moment

Brown University, 1971

When writing class was over, several of
my earnest students lingered, those who knew
they really weren't doing all I wanted,
and wanted to, but couldn't find their way.
What I tried to tell them, always, was
to dare some kind of greatness. Timid with
their feelings, they supposed a navigation
in roiling depths where they were barely wading.
No point in putting it to them like that:
perceived insult would only blunt the message.

They clustered round me as I walked outside,
still asking questions, followed down the green
under the arch to Thayer Street. I stopped
and pointed at the studio art building,
converted from an old garage, across
the street. Long slated to be razed, its time
had come. The dozers had already bitten
deep into its far corner, before lunch
imposed a brief reprieve. Equipment sat
untended, silent – shortly to resume;
before nightfall the building would be down.

"We'll never have a better chance than this,"
I said, and led them, puzzled, to the site.
Its southern wall a checkerboard of panes,
rectangles set in metal frames, its glass
a glint repeated in the light of noon,
the structure, momentarily intact,

cried out a teaching moment. I reached down
and fetched up from the crushed stone underfoot
a handful. Windows hardly thirty feet
from where I stood could not be missed. The crash
of breaking glass is like a crunching bell,
and soon my students stood on either side
and slung their stones as though each shattered pane
rang out the end of class. We kept it up
until no window in that wall was left
unbroken. Giddy, satisfied, the students
all went off grinning. I was smiling too:
although I'd never set foot in that building,
I knew (I'd seen a yearbook photograph)
someone had painted on an inside wall
"Caution is the enemy of art,"
from Motherwell, who added, "Everyone
is more cautious than he thinks he is."

A Whitman Update

In his time Whitman flung his filament
out into the vast oceans of space
to catch his isolated soul somewhere,
to bridge the spheres. And other poets spun
from out of their imagination one
created as their perfect counterpart,
unrealizeable, who could inspire
their greatest exercise, and would suffice
to keep them working on in isolation.

Today we launch electric filaments
that speed across the vacant vast surrounding
and tirelessly seek to make connection.
Now we can reach beyond the veil and find,
at last, that one who understands us as
we've always wished: without approximation,
reproof, or ignorance; who accepts all.

If that were so, we might behave with grace;
instead a name, a face, a footprint on
the earth replaces our imagination,
imposing the impossibilities
of living with the real. Better the dream.

An Audience of One

West Dennis, Mass. 1975

Appearing at The Columns on the Cape,
Clark Terry's in the middle of his set.
His solo on "I Want a Little Girl,"
ebullient as usual, spills out
a bushel of joy in clusters of plump notes
juicy in their skins, alive and shading
in rich cry. Done, he turns back to the vocal,
light and careful, standing at the mike;
he's set up on the floor, so close to one
small table he can bend down to the lone
fan so keen for such proximity.

And when he gets to *"I don't even care..."*
that's just what he does. Instead of singing
the next line, he leans and whispers something
into his listener's ear. The fan cracks up,
and like a nuclear reaction so
do all the people in the club at once:
a memory like a rimshot for the crowd
to carry home. For me – I was the fan –
I had to laugh when Clark bent down to me
and shared this secret – "...wouldn't care if she
wasn't wearing nothing but a slip!"

"As a Man Is, So He Sees"

The shaving mirror nailed below the eaves
to scatter last year's woodpecker in fright
at the appearance of its magnified
and sudden lookalike, benignly tilts
this Spring beside the robin's nest, assembled
where side wall meets the downspout's crook. Serene,
the mother bird keeps watch all day beneath
a great-eyed Presence, calming and protective;
she feels herself repeated in its image.

At the Beach

Right now the clouds, swift-moving, all are somewhere
else, the breeze has lulled, the sun direct
above this quiet spot, drenching the beach
in blocks of color clear, sharp-lined, concise.
Meanwhile on blankets, hiding in a bunch,
the young are trying things they've heard about,
or seen, believing lies their bodies tell them.

Girls have studied closely how to look
while peeling off their shirts, the crossing of
the hands over the head, the languid tug,
and how to drop and step out of their jeans.
They barter what they have, extending credit
as expectations fluctuate, and prices
plunge or spike by dint of ignorance.

Boys, reduced to parts, know what to do
but not the way they'll feel – and showing what
you feel, they've learned, just leads to complications.
Better to act and not to question why,
and don't boys all want one thing, anyway?

The sea looks calm; the waves nibble a bit
along the margin, up and down the shore.
The water is inviting – placid, warm
up to your knees. You see down to the bottom,
or so it seems, until the undertow
sucks at your heels; and if you let it go
it pulls you out beyond the barrier,
its voice, at first a whisper, deafening.

Black and Tan Fantasy

Trumpeter Bubber Miley's plunger mute style helped to give Duke Ellington's band in the Twenties its distinctive "Jungle Band" sound. "Black and Tan Fantasy" was a signature example.

As soon as Bubber's growling filled the room
the seventh grade boys started twitching in
their seats. "That sounds like it's for strippers!" one
piped up impishly. I tried to save
the moment.
                    "Well, it's true that Ellington
wrote this music for dancers, but they didn't –"
He'd already jumped up from his chair
and started miming to the music, knees
and elbows swaying.
                    I regarded him
with a mild eye, often seen in one
perusing a familiar menu, but
made no remark. New at my teaching job,
hired for high school but begged to try
one period of middle schoolers by
this private school's headmaster, I'd agreed
reluctantly to take a music class
for just one day. One would be all it took.

Within what seemed like seconds, an audition
for a Hoochy Coochy Chorus Line was in
full swing, with every boy a writhing star.
I stood and watched them, clearly unimpressed.
They kicked it up a notch and in a minute
fifteen shirts were on the floor. My face
was bland; the music, guttural, strode on.

The pants came next, and when I didn't turn
a hair, the rest – until the room was filled,
like any locker room, with naked boys.

I looked at them. The music stopped. I paused
and said "What are you going to do now?"
They looked around, collected up their clothes,
put them back on, and sat down in their seats,
their heads, if not hung down, a little lower.

The thing is, never give them what they want.

Black Pearls, 1942

"Tell him about the black pearls."
                          "What?"
                                        "The pearls
that you won in the Service, on the boat."

"I won them in a crap game two days out
of Fiji. There was nothing else to do
on board ship, that's all. I couldn't miss
that night."
                "How many were there?"
                                          "I don't know,
a handful."
                "Of black pearls? Do you know how
much they'd be worth now? How did you lose them?"

"I didn't say I lost them."
                      "So you gave
them to those Island girls then, didn't you?"

My father looked annoyed but didn't fight it;
I'd seen the yellowed snapshots, half-clad girls
on either arm, no less, him grinning in
a sawtooth skirt like native men on Fiji.

"You should have brought them back for me," my mother
said. My father got a little nettled.

"We didn't know where they were sending us,"
he said, "we could have been dead the next day."

"But you weren't," my mother went on, "so
you could have brought them back. A handful of

~28~

black pearls!" Her eyes were glittering. "You should
have given them to me."

"And how was I
supposed to do that when I hadn't even
met you yet?" my Dad said, half-triumphant.

With arched eyebrow and quick move of a hand
she dismissed him. "Never mind about
that. You should have given them to me."

Bossa Antigua

*"The Advanced LIGO laboratories in the US have traced
the warping of space from the merger of two black holes about
1.3 billion light-years from Earth. It represents the last great
confirmation of Einstein's ideas, and opens the door to a completely
new way to investigate the universe."*

Jonathan Amos, BBC News, February 11, 2016

The market, volatile, was down today;
the mercury will plummet overnight
into the single digits. Candidates
in the Granite State were separated
by tenths of a percentage point in seeking
a temporary job. This bump I hear
amid a roar like breakers on a shore
began a billion years ago and reached
us just in time to prove Einstein was right
predicting it a hundred years ago.

It had to wait for us to build an ear
fine to the rhythm as two black holes samba
until they eat each other up: this bossa
antigua, a new music of the spheres,
names the next wave from this moment on.

Cans on the Shelf

Once that shelf is full, if I put one
more can up there, another one will fall.
I won't know which until it hits the floor.

I could control what's added and what's lost
if I could bring myself to take one down,
but I don't want to say which one I like
more than another. So instead of choosing
I keep hoping I can have them all.

Christmas Morning in Rumford, 2012

As though the children's wishes made last night
could carry weight to freight the clouds in rising
(so many trained not to expect too much
by recent outcomes), in response the least
to claim the name of snow has settled on
the landscape of this Christmas, barely white.

Counting Without Numbers

for R.V.C.

 The fish tank stood beneath the stairs, across
from the front room. I'd never had a class
that met in the professor's house before
and made sure I arrived a little early.

He met me at the door, his manner coiled,
tense as a hand-bent spring, and led me to
the shining box of light and water, grinning.
The fish were darting in the tank. He threw
the first of many challenges to come
and said "How many?" with a glint of glee
bright behind the lenses of his glasses.

I looked. No fish would hold still long enough
to stay the counting; sudden scatter ruled.
I looked again and said "There's seventeen."
His grin pulled even wider then: I knew
what seventeen fish looked like in a tank.

He came to teach me how to write a novel –
that what you drafted first, however sure
of what you were about, how clean your plan,
you had to read a finished manuscript
to find the real, elusive story there
you weren't aware of telling; then to pitch
the rest away, and start from next to scratch
again – to wrestle with the deepest self
you could engage, and not release your hold
except it blessed. I flourished in the method
in the life that's followed, grateful that I learned
to count without numbers, and plan alike.

Dark Certainties

Retired, disconsolate at sixty, he
feels himself a kind of flea, and thinks
his long career uninterrupted sucking
of blood close to the surface of life's neck,
valuing his contribution less
than a pin's fee. After he has stepped away
he's kept up his consumption of the rare
expensive goods and services designed
to flatter by their acquisition, but
he draws no pleasure from them, nor from travel,
which occupies him with its needed planning,
execution, and recovery.

He describes these symptoms of self-loathing
with resignation, but with rueful tone
enough for me to ask off-handedly
if he's considered volunteering – he
has time, an expertise, and many he could help –
but sadly he protests, without surprise,
that he's already tried: no one will take him.

As one who delicately blows above
the ashes of a burned out fire, in hopes
of drawing up a hidden spark which might
remain, I show the barest of concern
in testing out the depths of his despair
from one direction, gently, then another.
But he will not be comforted. He takes
the taste of iron in his mouth for justice.
Whoever taught him punishment has trained
him to continue it now they are gone.

Complicit with the source, he seamlessly
conceals it from himself; unworthiness
becomes his self-fulfilling condemnation.
Dark certainties, impenetrable, slick
as black obsidian, slope over me –
hope of redemption finds no foothold here.
Say what you will about belief; it may
be insufficient, but it's necessary.

Demand, then Supply

A gift wrought by a blacksmith drinking buddy
who knows that I write songs, the feeder stands
upright beyond my kitchen window, hammered
into the yielding ground. Its iron forms
a staff, its five lines open to the sky
in Vs providing trenches for the seed
and room for neighbor birds to perch and feed,
each body one plump note; each group suggests
a melody my friend hoped might inspire.

Faithful for a time, I filled the troughs
as jays and cardinals splashed their color down
and bobbed to peck and start, then dart away.
They showed me music as they chirped their own;
I welcomed company. But as it will,
life intruded, and I lapsed, as winters
flared and drove the birds away. I let
the staff stand empty by its hand-cut clef.

Years later, in December, I'm surprised
to hear a battery of birdsong twitter
outside my window. Is it out of hope
or memory that they return, despite
the seasons of neglect, or is it need
so desperate they clutch at any trace
of mortal questions answered, once, for others?

Reminded of the ways of inspiration,
I find the bag of seed right where I left it.
I feed them, then sit down to write the poem.

Diagnostic

I'd pushed the button; trouble was to come –
continue, rather – in another form.
Our love of several years had dried, its course
changed far upstream, nearer an unseen source,
and now we gulped at dust with every breath.

Impossible in person, still we tried to phone
only to find our words clotting the line
between the silences. That faith bled out
that makes communication possible,
we'd fall to disagreeing over what
was said two sentences before. And so,
supposing it might help to know for sure,
I'd pushed the button on the old machine
that said *two way record*, and went on talking,
trying to forget the tape was running,
knowing soon enough we'd hit the wall
without a special effort on my part.

A minute, maybe two, was all it took
for us to fall into the pattern, starting
with "that's not what I meant" and ending with
"No, that's not what I said." We'd always prized
a rational discussion, and it seemed
to me quite reasonable to suggest
we just go back and listen to the tape.

That's when the trouble changed. When I explained
we had a reference we could consult,
reliable beyond dispute, to show
objectively what each of us had said,

~37~

what followed the sharp silence on the line
was nothing like a word of thanks. I was
upbraided, my betrayal was denounced,
my solemn promise instantly demanded:
I must destroy the tape. I must not listen
to it, and it must be done the moment
that this call was ended. These requirements
were unrelated to forgiveness, which
in any case remained unlikely; they
were non-negotiable and mandatory.

This happened, long ago. I tell the story
to prepare you for a simple test. No, really –
may I have a show of hands? Do you
believe I a) destroyed the tape as promised,
not checking it to see if I'd been right;
or b) destroyed it, after listening;
or c) kept it and listen when I please?
What kind of person am I, would you say?
So, hands for a? For b? And now for c?

Thanks. What have we learned about ourselves?

~38~

Disturbing the Peace

The dust lies in a settled layer
on every knickknack in the hutch,
and at my age I hardly dare
disturb a surface very much.

That just brings on a fit of sneezing
which I'd much rather do without,
and I find cleanliness less pleasing
now that the truth about it's out:

Clean doesn't last, but dirty does;
as soon as you complete the chore
that dust resettles where it was,
and all is as it was before.

So learn the lesson you've been shown –
try leaving well enough alone.

Dotting the Eye

*The total eclipse of the sun on March 7, 1970 was visible
on most of the Eastern coast of the US.*

The recesses of space provide the scene:
the principals a bone-cold, airless moon,
a furious incinerating sun
which eats itself into a pouring shine.

Their play a mediation between light
and dark which scores a line of shadow on
the surface of the turning earth, its first
landfall in Mexico, then east-northeast
across the Caribbean, bending up
through Florida, and then along the coast
as though to satisfy the human eyes
turned toward the skies on up to Nova Scotia.

This interaction of great silent orbs
goes unnoticed half a world away
in Southeast Asia, where an open conflict
exerts a sway, invisible, within
those youths about to reach maturity
back in the States. Each struggles with the issues:
to serve, or to refuse, or to evade;
to take the place of someone who enjoys
a privilege because you lack it; or
to use advantage, putting someone else
at risk – and once resolved, each choice emerges
from a private place into a public action.

*As darkness scours the landscape, he looks up
and covers his left eye. The ring of light*

~40~

is chaste at first, an edge for precious seconds;
then it bulges out in a fierce gem
that swells intensity. He stares as blankly
as he can and takes care not to blink.
Light's needle pierces to the retina
where no pain receptors are, and does
its work — a pin point's worth of rods and cones
are burned away like unsuspecting ants
in the remorseless beam of a boy's glass.

In years to come he navigates with ease
necessities of sight in daily life.
Should he cover his left eye while reading,
the blind spot in the center of his right
shows him a blank instead of any word
he tries to focus on. It reappears
with help from his undamaged other eye.
So only if required to use the sights
of any of the issued weapons (which
the government elected not to do)
would he find each target vanishes.

Flaming Youth

Crack of the bat, I know I'll never catch it.
Turn and take off, straight back in deep center.
No fence on this field, the only hope
is pick it off the ground and hit the cut.
Stride after stride I go, head down, speed-blind.
Hopeless I know, stride after stride. I throw
my arm up straight, glove open, backhand turned.
Ball smacks dead on, zero in the pocket.

For S.S.

He strikes, his mind at every stroke a hit;
sips at facility, and keeps a case of it.
And he has whimsy, yes, to salt his wit;
but faith – alas, the lad hath not a bit.

Geode

Big as a baby's head, ribbed as a bubbled cloud,
its amber chalcedony shell conceals
transparent quartz or purple amethyst.
Years in its making number in the millions
as buried deep in sediment it ripened,
ground water trickling its contribution.

It's bored a bullet's path for fifty years
straight through the quiet haven of my life;
its secret colors hid in darkness still
will go on undisturbed when I am dust.

It's safe with me; I raise no hammer to
its mystery, imagining inside
a host of tinted possibilities.
I'd rather keep them all alive at once
than break it open, killing all but one.

Grand Canal, August 1972

Amid the splendor-in-decay of Venice,
as water laps against the gondola,
in company of strangers, stranger still:
her gaze, surrounded by arresting features
ageless, exquisite, locks on to mine
outside of time, and seals the world away.

In ornate frames, two mirrors face to face.

He Is As the Wind

To one I was a source of agitation
in aspen leaves beyond her window glass,
insistent whispers, keeping her from sleep.

Another felt me rising suddenly
under darkened skies, signaling rain,
not to be trusted with one open shutter.

To this one, twister, unpredictable,
which drives her underground, its path a risk
to pluck her house up whole into the vortex.

To that one, elemental, merciless
in its intensity, which scours out
the prairie, bringing her to desperation.

To this one, welcome breath of freshening
after a long, confining season in
the cold and dark; it stirs, and she throws open

wide the doors and windows, and allows it
to lick all surfaces, and change the air
within, then buttons all up tight again.

Where is that one to whom I am no less
a need than breathing, nor no more a threat
than exhalation warm against her neck?

He Learns a Lesson from a Star-Crossed Letter

Brown University, Spring 1967

A stack of books came rumbling down the chute
and tumbled in the bin to top the pile.
I sat unseen inside an office room
that housed the catalogue of paper cards,
one to each book that had been out on loan.
My job was matching books to proper cards;
I picked up the first book and opened it,
and as I did a letter fluttered out,
fell to the floor next to my foot, face up.

The envelope was neatly slit, as though
it was worth saving. On the front I saw
her name, and the return address from her
home town. Through freshman fall and winter, she'd
told me about her hometown high school beau;
though she and I were going out, her glowing
tales of him kept me at bay. And here
he was, in his own voice at last: a gift
from the unnamed and minor deity
in charge of distant lovers' correspondence.

And did I think to give it back unread?
I did. I saw no clean and simple outcome.
The way that I'd obtained it might be questioned,
my motives scrutinized. Would she believe
I hadn't read it, opened as it was,
and from a rival I might never meet
on more revealing terms? Better to say
nothing at all, then. And could I resist

~47~

the chance to see him as he was, and read
of them in the original, instead
of her translation? I could not resist.

Did I ignore my violation? Yes.
Was I prepared to dislike him? Of course.
But he was not at all what I expected.
Tentative and insecure, he tried
to keep some hold over their present by
reminders of their past. And he had questions
about his unknown college rival. Why
would she reveal so little? Who was he?
And were they close? He felt so far away.

I never got to say what I had learned –
secrets which I had no right to know
and couldn't have explained. But after that.
whenever she brought up her high school beau,
I kept calm, never rising to the bait.

His Daemon Tells It Like It Is

I don't concern myself much with the human
who is my instrument. I interrupt
his days with words and music, lend a sense
of form, and he forgets to eat and sleep.

He thinks that he and I are one; believes
he needs acknowledgment at most, at least
attention, for the works I put through him
and put him through. Although he is my thrall

he wants to be loved just as though he acted
on his own; it matters to him that
he gets what he deserves, and doesn't suffer.
In the greater scheme it's not important.

Hope Speaks

*Hesiod's 8th century BC account of the Pandora myth uses
the word "pithos," which was a large storage jar; it was mis-
taken for the word for "box" in the later Latin translation.*

I was a wedding gift, enclosed within
a jar of bronze, unbreakable, and sealed
for safe delivery, roomy enough
to store great quantities of grain or oil,
or even house alive or dead a man
driven to such lengths by poverty.

It served me well at first, until a host
of ills were crammed in with me, close, contentious,
each struggling with its neighbor to control
the space. I was compressed, forced to a corner,
deprived of air and light. A hive of evils
buzzed above me; silenced, I endured
the trip, alone among them all in bearing
welcome.

        Once she lifted up the lid
they swarmed the woman, stinging every inch
they found exposed, bowing her down beneath
the weight of sickness, toil, and pain they brought,
frenzy the sole attention left to them
to pay in place of gratitude. Bedeviled,
bitten raw, she howled and hugged the floor,
hiding her face from furious assault.

I hide as well within the emptied jar,
by this bronze lid I'm powerless to move,

~50~

and know how much she needs me; I call out
to her to free me, but she hesitates.

Against her will she must approach again
the source of all her troubles, open up
to all its possibilities, and dare
to let me out. I call to her, and wait.

How I Learned About Aging

I used to like to hollow out a pepper,
raw, green, and glossy; fill it to the brim
with orange juice, and drink, and bite a ring
around the rim, and drink, and bite again
until both drink and glass were gone, and no
cleanup was necessary. I was just
a kid, but I'd finessed the question of
the glass half-full or -empty. Up until
I drained the last drop, it was always full.

How I Learned About Leadership

Fort Leonard Wood, Missouri, October 1970

In AIT my squad leader got sick
with spinal meningitis; his stripped bunk
was all we ever learned about his fate.
The sergeants made me squad leader that day.
I hadn't asked for it and wasn't free
to refuse. Each morning I was told
to pick three men for detail. There were ten
besides me in the squad: three were good workers
who didn't need a supervisor; four
would do a decent job if you were watching;
three would try to hide, get nothing done
at all unless you rode them every second.
Results were barely satisfactory.
They wore you out with their malingering.

The Army could be pleased, and my days easy:
just pick the same three guys who did good work
each day. Or I could make my life a grind:
be vigilant, cajole, coerce, subdue;
for all pains taken, average results.
Except for being fair to everyone.

How I Learned About Omertá

"One day a big stone came down from the mountain.
It rolled into the one road in the village
and stopped right in the middle of the street.
It was so big the wagons with the cheese
all made a line and couldn't get around it.
What did the people do?"

                              My Nannu smiled.
He finished with a swallow the last inch
of homemade muscatel left in his glass
and placed it back down on the kitchen table.

I thought awhile and said, "They dragged it off?"

"It was too big. The *scheccudeddus* couldn't
pull it," he said, and grinned. I was expected
to keep on answering.

                         "They broke it up?"
I said, my kid's brow creased from heavy thinking.

"It was too hard. The hammers only bounced
off and the sparks jumped, but it wouldn't break,"
he said, and watched me carefully.

                                   I said
"Did they put water on it, and at night
after it froze, the ice in any cracks
expanded, and it split apart in pieces?"

There was a wrinkle in *his* brow. "It was

too smooth," he said, and smiled and shook his head.
"But that's a good guess. You know what they did?"

"I give up," I said, and sat up straight.

"They buried it," he said, and gave me time
to think about what kind of stone he meant.

How I Learned About Self-Determination

September 11, 2015

The period began just after nine
that Tuesday. Students tumbled in in knots
as usual, before the bell, but lacked
that energy, so skittery and edgy,
expected from ninth graders, new to school,
each other, adolescence, to themselves.

Instead there roiled unspoken currents in
the room. It bumped and bubbled like a lid
that barely caps a full pot's rolling boil,
an energy I'd never felt before
in decades running class. They'd heard about
attacks, planes crashing, skyscrapers in flames
in New York, from TV news reports
in other classrooms; teachers had stopped class.
This was before all students had devices.
Not linked to cable, TVs sat on carts
with VCRs, without antennas. As
in my childhood, they got only four
stations. No matter – this would be on any.

They asked if we could watch the news instead
of having class. On any other day
that would have been a game to lure me off
my course. I would have smiled but gone ahead.

Today I acted differently. I asked
if any of them had a family member,
friend, or anyone they knew of, flying

in to New York that day. No one did.
I said then "If I put the TV on,
how long would it take for you to tell
if they're reporting something new, or if
they're just repeating what we've heard before?"

"A minute," someone said. They all agreed.
"All right," I said, "I'll put it on a minute.
You tell me if something new has happened.
If yes, we'll watch. If no, we're having class."

We watched. It was before the second plane
struck the South Tower, in that awful lull.
The kids said no; we turned off the TV,
the class becalmed, eye of the hurricane.

How I Learned About Signs from Above

Along the first base line, over the rail,
I'd lingered talking by the welcome tent
after the game began. A foul ball twisted
slowly, shallow, just above my head
and settled on the crushed stone just behind
me. Tracking after it a dozen steps,
I bent to snatch it up, exclaiming "got it!"

I saw out of the corner of my eye
a kid of ten in shorts and a team jersey,
running, just too late, his glove in hand.
"Want it?" I said. His face lit up. I flipped
it to him, straightened, and went back to finish
my conversation. A few minutes later,
it was time to find my seat. I had to walk
out of the park, around behind, and through
a parking lot to reach the gate. Mid-way
a ball sailed down and bounced in front of me,
and disappeared into the rows of cars.

I took it as a sign, but with a test.
I thought back to the knock of ball on asphalt,
wove my way in its direction, stepped
between the cars, along the memory,
after a minute thought of giving up;
accepted I must trust the moment. And
there it was, pure white with one dark scuff.

Until you do the work, it's not a sign.

How I Learned About Solitude

119 High St. Haverhill, Mass. 1951

I'm in the kitchen on the second floor.
My mother has just left. I'm three. I'm standing
between the stove and kitchen table, in
the middle of the floor. I take ten steps
and climb up on the chair next to the window.
I see my mother walk across the street
below me. Then she disappears. I know
there is a corner store two blocks away.
First time now I feel that I'm alone.
First time now, I feel that she'll be back.

I Play Roy Eldridge's Trumpet

Sandy's – Beverly, Mass. 1978

Pitted through its silver plate, and worn
down to the brass, the mouthpiece had held up
for him through the fierce hail of sessions since
the Thirties, as the horns had fallen from
his furious assault of breath. Pugnacious,
always ready for a challenge, Roy
had met the boppers on their native ground
and slung his winding phrases, serpent-like
in hiss and swing, over their fractured rhythms.
Unquenchable, his fiery spirit torched
on in the Seventies, the acid rasp
still smoking in his tone. At decade's end
well past sixty, in this club tonight,
he'd hurtled through his first set, heat undimmed.

When on the break I had been introduced
as a fellow trumpet player, and he'd seen
I had no horn with me, and needn't be
regarded as a rival spoiling for
a fight, he'd sat down, genial and easy
for some shop talk. "So tell me," he began
in his high, quick-and-ginger voice, "who do
you listen to? I mean, which trumpet players?"

"I'm a swing guy, Roy," I said. "I go
from Pops to you."

                            He peered up at me through
two roundish, thickened lenses. "Yeah," he said,
and grinned. "Me too."

                    Pleased then with how he'd put
the truth into a joke, he saw me steal
a look down at the trumpet cradled on
his knees, protected by his hand. How much
about him I could learn from its details!
Especially that mouthpiece, which I'd seen
on album cover photographs for years.
The cup configuration, from its depth
and shape, the bore and back bore, width
and rim – unyielding metal, yet caressed
in daily contact with the lips and breath:
a player's intimacy, personal
and secret, so close by.

                         Roy's eyebrows rose
a notch as he said, "Say, I've got to use
the can. Mind holding on to this awhile?"
And handed me his horn, and, nonchalant,
got up and walked away.

                         I felt its heft
for all of fifteen seconds then, before
I took it up, and placed my fingertips
against the valve caps, checked the dimpled cup,
and curious, grateful, brought it to my lips.

In Praise of Weakness

My vision isn't what it used to be;
my eyes supply a different clarity.
The surfaces, the edges in my room
no longer sharp, move more or less apart;
between, new figures find their way. Before,
forbidden any foothold in the world
beyond me, they remained within, without
a form. Deprived of signs, I stumbled in
the dark against their unseen presences.

Projected now around my view, about
private realities, they sound alarms;
my eyes supply a different clarity.
My vision isn't what it used to be.

In Single File

At the feeder's foot a square-tailed hawk
feasts on taken prey, sleek-headed; slopes
and picks at flesh, repeating, steeped in red.

Above, the neighbor birds still congregate,
indifferent to the act below, so close,
immediate, and deadly. Do they know
by wisdom of warm blood that they are safe
those moments Keen-Eyed Killer hoods his gaze,
distracted, while the sacrifice is done?

Indolence

Each day I feel I should do something more
to make me worthy of the high opinion
I'd like to have of how I've spent my life,
discounting what I may have done before.

The number of my days remaining may
be unknown, but they're diminishing
for sure, and yet I laze away the hours
and stubbornly refuse to get to work,

as though endless supplies made time so cheap
I could afford to shrug at squandering.
But like those Greeks who said "Nothing too much,"
I bring even anxiety to heel.

It Was Different in the Fifties

for Jack Connors

We like to say that life was simpler then,
but maybe gestures were just more direct.

A tree warden colleague of my father
in the Fifties, he was short and trim –
my father towered over him although
a mere five-ten himself – ruddy and brisk.
He'd have been in his sixties, in those days
when average men looked old at thirty-eight,
his face like Truman's only narrower.
He wore a gray fedora with a pinch
front and a teardrop crown outdoors, and lifted
it when inside, revealing thinning wisps
of white hair neatly combed across his scalp.

He was outgoing, vigorous, his mood
unfailingly upbeat. He'd seen worse times,
so he made no complaint. He liked to talk;
he'd say yes to a drink. When he shook hands
to say goodbye, he used a salesman's trick
which must have come straight out of the Depression:
his grip was moderate and firm, not held
too long, but just before he let you go
he squeezed you twice as hard, and held it for
a beat, as if to say "A man has got to find
a way to stand out in the world. You won't
forget me, if it's the last thing I do."

Johnny Hodges and Cleopatra

In Duke Ellington's group of tone parallels to Shakespearean characters, Such Sweet Thunder, *altoist Johnny Hodges played the part of Cleopatra in* "Half the Fun."

He, of that tone supreme which overwhelms
one's sense of sweetness, used to carry
colored bulbs and perfumes on the road,
replace the lights in hotel rooms and close
the blinds, dousing the variegated glass,
then laze back in the half-light on the bed.
Hot reds and blues infused the space with scent
then, dense and rich, embodying his moods.

So taken with him was I in those days
I first was flooded by his graceful shaping,
his aerial swoops and plunges in the sharp
joy of his cry, I never stopped to think
how else the perfume was a help, to mask
the acrid smells of substances which let
him stay the chaos of the life outside
and drowse at deeper levels of the dream.

Beauty's both sublime and practical:
like Cleopatra, who, servants revealed,
secreted potent perfumes in a certain
place within her body, so bad air
in passing through and out of her was sweet.

JR Declines a Camping Invitation

"I hate Nature. I hate bugs and trees.
Give me the pavement, in the neighborhood."

Learning the Wall

When Dent hit the ball, I looked at Yaz,
patrolling left field as he had before,
spelling an injured Rice. From my six dollar
walk up bleacher seat I saw the wall
at my right hand, and knew how well he played it:
years had taught him all the dings and angles,
wind direction factored against height,
all the tricks the wall would use to lead
the fielder in too close or too far back.
Yaz would know; no need to watch the ball.
I saw him take a few steps to his right,
look up, and suddenly he crumpled down
into a one-knee crouch. The ball was gone.

A Mozart lifetime later, as I watch
a Youtube doc on Fenway history,
I see Dent's swing again, from closer up,
and suddenly the camera cuts away;
the face of one fan fills the screen, to stand
for universal dismay. It is mine.

The expression on my youthful face,
not sad so much as marveling at what
the Irish call "the music of what happens,"
looks at me through time as if to say
that gain and loss are not the point, as they
will come. My job must be to look away,
not waiting for the outcomes; rather, live
so as to learn the wall so well that I
can see, before it happens, what will be.

Learning to Hear

The bumping needle drop was audible
throughout the classroom. Then the low hiss started,
followed by the stately theme of plucked
strings, dulled, descending on the old recording.

The children had been asked to listen, nothing
more. After the piece was done we filled
the blackboard with a list of words to capture
what they'd heard. Not one said "harpsichord,"
"Scarlatti," or "Landowska." Not one knew
what old recordings sounded like. We talked
about the phonograph and how it was
invented. Then I played the cut again.

"Guess when this was made," I said. We filled
the board again with years, most wildly off
the mark. "The year," I said, "was nineteen-forty,
the place was Paris. Listen one more time."

Two minutes in, a few noticed the thumps,
three in a row. Nobody knew about
the Spring invasion, Paris put at risk,
the boom of anti-aircraft fire outside
the studio that penetrated through
the walls to find its way into the groove.

"Not long after this," I said, "Landowska
had to flee the country. She left Paris
with two suitcases. After that her house
was looted and destroyed; she never lived
in France again. Just think," I said, "while she

was playing, bombs were going off. She could
have died. Would you be scared? Now see if you
can hear her fingers falter – does she flinch
or hesitate?" I played it once again.

"It's the music on her mind," I said
once the cut was done. "Only the music.
Now we've all heard the music through four times.
The sound you heard each time, identical.
But then you learned about who made the sound,
the world it came into, how it was made.
And every time you heard a little more.
Why? It stays the same – but you are different."

"Lest You Dash Thy Foot Against a Stone"

Now along their worn grain, blanched to dun,
the dowel ladder rungs bit at my arches
so I pulled harder on the side rails with
my stubby hands and arms, uneasy by
the third step though my Uncle braced the way.
A kid afraid of heights, I needed curing.

He'd led me to the big shed by the house,
its nearly flat roof eight feet off the ground.
When I had clambered up into a crouch
he followed, said to stand up straight, and walked
me to the back edge. Black nubbed shingles crunched
under my steps. I shied as I approached it;
he stood behind me, took me by the shoulders,
said, "Step up. Put your toes across the line –
I've got hold of you. Look down." I saw
my sneakers, then the edge, then ground below.
He took away his hands. I felt as though
my body swayed in high and shifting winds.

I looked then, farther off, across the land
behind the house. The green grape arbor built
by my Sicilian grandfather from pipes
and lattice-work was densely grown, rough leaves
and twisting tendrils thick with bitter fruit
but true to its purpose, dark and cool beneath.
I saw it from above now, different:
in brilliant sunlight lacy and complex,
a puzzle of impenetrable pieces.

Earth is too strong for us. We've struck a bargain
with it: we need time to moderate,

subdue the fierce expression of its love.
We live in a slow fall to its embrace.

That day a kid was standing on a roof;
one step would bring earth in a sudden rush.
I was right to fear the step. I backed away;
declared I'd learned what I had come for. Then
taking my time I climbed down to the ground,
resuming the long business of living,
to have not everything as we would wish –
sweet grapes, mild nights, the open palm of day –
instead to win some respite from the fists
of a relentless sun, a place to sit
with friends beneath the cooling vines and clusters:
such mercies as we earn by way of toil
before we settle back to earth.

                              Since then
I've lived another sixty years, and made
my way to other heights. As I look down
I see what bears me up: that I've been lifted
by love of others, leafy green, protective,
entwined and rooted, bole and branch, between
the ground and me – that earth curls up
to meet, and make, another puzzle piece.
The sunlight dazzles, clarifies the landscape,
warms me now as I resume my climb,
my footing sure, my life beneath my feet,
no longer needing to be cured; instead,
to start from higher. Now I rise to fly.

Licking the Beater

Whipped until it stiffened and stood up
in frothy tufts above the curves, the cream
is sweet against my tongue's tip, yielding more
than soft-serve till the blades resist. I curl
around the ridges, slip the surfaces
to their convergence, fetching the confection
eagerly above, below, along its length,
and lolling as I go, licking it clean.

Locks and Doors

For David Cashman

The closed door of your poem "Warped and Binding,"
stuck against the balky lock you set
with an unpracticed hand so long ago
on a forgotten date, remembers for you
now its first conditions, yielding, when
they coincide today, without a struggle.

You're moved to fashion metaphor, and use
Jesus the carpenter of air to gentle
up the opening, only to say
how different most days are in bringing weather
we are not at home in, where the door's
warp forces us at best to keep within.

The door of metaphor itself allows
such different entry! For how easily
the meaning moves, a fluid through the forms,
and we can be at once inside and out.

Last night I woke up at the deepest hour
to feel a tongue of cold air licking at
my cheek, and rose to shuffle through the chill
out to my front room, where the door stood open
to the night drafts of December, though its
latch bolt still was locked, its striking plate
and face plate both undamaged. I was left
to wonder how the wind had worked its will;
an endless gentle pressure urged its way

around what would have stopped a push or pull,
however violent, and penetrated
the barrier without making a click.

So what am I to make of locks and doors?
Better to be a carpenter of air.

Maya's First Hard Boiled Egg

Set down by Mother, in a rush, the brown
egg wobbled drunkenly around the dish,
skidded as Maya brought her finger down
to poke it – it would take a special wish

to make it small enough to fit her face,
and not too hard for baby teeth to bite.
Her older brother, watching from his place
across the kitchen table, to incite

his sister's tears, piped up in impish glee
"Betcha can't make it stand up on end."
She tried it as he grinned in mockery:
each end up, she couldn't comprehend

why every time she took her hand away
the top would lose its balance and descend,
and once again she'd look on in dismay.
Her brother saw no reason to extend

her agitation. With a gallant reach
across the table, and a knowing smirk,
he said "Okay, now watch – I'm gonna teach
you how. Here's all it takes to make it work."

With that, he raised the egg and brought it down,
and cracked the big end on the table top.
It stood in fractured majesty. The frown
on Maya's face transformed into a drop

at first, and then a torrent, of her tears.
Fetched by her daughter's cries, Mother surveyed

the damage on the table. There are fears
not only groundless, but a grace displayed

upon a transformation of our sight.
"It's busted," Maya sobs. "Oh, honey, no —"
her Mother says, "It's not. It's still all right.
It's just this broken shell that's got to go."

Her practiced hands remove the covering.
The egg, unshelled, is placed back on the plate,
its white on white, an unmasked lover hovering
above the surface of its unlike mate.

Maya's expression quiets down to mild:
she sees a vapor round the white orb wreathing
warm against the china dish. The child,
eyes wide in wonder, coos out "Look — it's breathing."

Misdirection of the Natural World

The pearl, though grateful for its grit
takes pains to keep concealing it.

Mistaken Notions of the Dead

I call him Ned though that was not his name.
He was a solitary, on the fringe
with college roommates, quiet in the din.
He stayed in town after we graduated;
running into him was mildly awkward;
though he was thoughtful and approved of jokes,
he'd pause in conversation, tilt his head,
and looking off into the middle distance
"O" his lips, sometimes for thirty seconds
before he said a word. He was convinced
late in the seventies, that if elected,
Ronald "Ray-Gun" would destroy the world
to root out Communism. There was nothing
you could say to make him stop repeating
it. He liked to wear a shirt that said
Never Enough across the chest, in letters
big above the *Baking Company*.

I didn't see him for a while, and learned
he'd killed himself before Election Day
in '80. I thought back then, to the last
time we'd talked. We'd met by accident
along the sidewalk on a narrow street
downtown. He'd dipped his head from side to side
and brought it up to look at me directly:
he'd read about a murder in the papers.
Police were looking for a suspect, thought
to be a certain age, height, size and features
not unlike his own. He was convinced
he was their target; in the article
the vague description was deliberate,

~79~

to give him a false sense of ease. But he
knew better. They were after him, he said;
the words shot out like lighthouse beams, the flashing
regular and monotone, his face
flat in mid-grimace, tight against his teeth,
the lack of any pause a tell-tale sign.
Nothing I said could talk him down to reason.

Morning Glory

Waking up alone just after dawn,
she feels the pillow next to hers. The deep
impression of his head has cooled. She rolls
up out of bed, goes over to the window,
pulls back the curtain, looks down at the driveway
just brightening below. The Bronco's gone,
his throwdown getaway with the roof racks.
He's left the Escalade to her. It has
the kiddy seat. She hears their daughter breathe,
asleep across the hall, and feels a pang –
abandoned. Yes, it must be. And she'd known
for weeks something was coming, by the way
he'd made each normal move deliberate.

But part of her resists. Some other reason
for leaving before Saturday begins –
it's possible, she thinks. It could be he'll
be back with milk and waffles by the time
we'd all be getting up. She has to know;
she holds back her emotions long enough
to check the airline luggage in the closet.
It's there. She struggles to convince herself
that all still can be well, but there's a doubt –
it's caught down in her throat and won't be swallowed.

There's one place left, she thinks, the leather bag
he wouldn't throw out from his father's things
after we broke the house up, it's upstairs
in the left attic room. That suitcase has
some kind of special meaning for him. Up
she goes; the seldom-walked-on steps creak out

~81~

a protest. He'd have woke me up for sure,
she thinks, if he'd come up here. At the top
she turns left on the landing, lifts the latch
and edges sideways through the narrow door,
its white paint thick with layers, past the stacks
of boxed up Christmas lights and ornaments,
the bolts of fabric. Over by the eaves
she ducks her head and looks under the window.
The morning light is slanting, cool, and brilliant.

The dust is undisturbed and thick beside
the wall, except for a neat rectangle on
the floor. The dark hardwood gleams fresh inside.
A drop blooms darker in it. Then another.

Mushroom Hunters, 1957

They wore earth tones, deep tans and saddle leather
taupes along with bat-gray, and the standby
blacks of stockings tightly sleek, kerchiefs
that cowled their broad-brushed, animated features:
Old World women and their men, coarse-vested,
arms in rolled up sleeves, home-cobbled boots
with soles the thickness of their thumbs, went out
together in a group on Saturdays
into the woods, brown grocery bags in hand
to hunt wild mushrooms, as they used to do
in Sicily. Old Country woods and New,
not quite alike, still yielded much the same,
and though I was a child and uninvited
I wondered how the wisdom carried over
that led them to the aspens, oaks, or birches
which sheltered, huddled at their bases, all
the rich array of fungi that they prized.

Did they amuse themselves, imagining
that they were young again, those friends, long-standing
bootstrap immigrants, on foot along
familiar childhood paths? Did they tell stories,
sing, exchange old gossip? I imagined
finding the favored objects of their search
conferred a comfort deep and reassuring:
Old Country truths still served them in the new.

For all that mushroom gathering was hidden
from me at nine, I'd see when they returned
their treasure: secret creatures swelled at midnight,
heavy with their oily essences
which stained the paper bags in dark, wet circles
everywhere they touched. When tumbled out

across the kitchen counter, plumped up dreams
or languid fancies, visible, could not
have stupefied like these, stubby and hunched,
buff-domed, or tendril-tall and gently turned
with undersides close-vaned and delicate,
still dressed in clinging flecks of moist black earth
and borrowed colors, here and there exploding
in flaring ochres or smooth bluish-black.

Into a pot of water they would go
then, with a shiny silver Walking Liberty
half dollar. Heated to a rolling boil,
they'd surface, bobbing in a group, their tones
slick and muted. Strained off, they would sit
while my Nana dumped the water out
and fished up the bright disc. Initiate
to mysteries, she knew: a blackened coin
meant poison, and the trove went in the bucket.

Today I read that test is false, a folk
tradition born in superstition, thought
true because experience led the hunters
to make safe choices. Current wisdom warns
that look-alikes in a new country may
deceive and threaten, deadly, though the coin
comes clean. Our halves today, bled of their silver,
no longer speak; they lack their audience.

Experience hints to us still of danger.
But in today's world, look-alikes, more norm
than rare exceptions, rule, and springing up
in darkness overnight in thick profusion
crowd out our comfort with familiar truths.
Where is our testing coin, and the belief
that lets us trust a search in unknown regions,
in friendly and long-standing company?

My Bow Ties

Navy pin-dot sprigs on pure white silk;
Bright and brighter stars on pitch-blue black.

Known for my hand-tied bow ties, I could go
for weeks without repeating. People said
they'd never seen such ties before. In fact,
each one was hand made and unique, the group
created by a mother and a son:
one to envision, one to realize.

A patch of melody along a staff,
inverted through the knot, against straw-yellow.

Expert with fabric, needle, shears, and thread,
Mom could have executed any plan,
but she had no idea what I'd wear.
We'd look at bolts of cloth, and I'd imagine
patterns with the weave or on the bias.
Some cultivated silk, too slick or thin,
would stretch, and needed backing, stitched on first
then turned, its outside in, to swell the knotting.

Ripe, tiny strawberries strewn on green cotton.
Scattered black oak leaves stacked grey on grey.

One piece whose pattern drifted lazily
I had her cut haphazardly. It made,
depending on the side against the neck
and end crossed over first, four different bows.

She'd gone against her instincts, but admitted
that trusting me was right: it was our best.

Cross-hatched gold strokes engraved on midnight black;
I choose according to my mood. Today,
a box of crayons spills across my throat.

Nightlight

The luminescent stars above my bed
I stuck up on the ceiling one by one
when I first bought this house glow down on me
with light they soaked up from my reading lamp.
Poor temporary evocation of
real stars, they're still a modest homemade comfort
although they fade before I fall asleep.

As if each one were someone I have loved
and haven't seen for years, imagination
brightens for a brief few moments with
the glow of their emotion should we meet –
warmth, regret, nostalgia, guilt, relief –
then they recede into the general darkness.

Not Lost, Found

Discovered in a wooden case I saved
out of my parents' house after they passed,
this snapshot captures perfectly the scene:
Saint Anthony procession, nineteen-fifty.
In the background two white-shirted men
shoulder the litter on stout poles. The saint
stands on the platform they support, with lilies
around his feet to mark his purity.
He holds a book; the Christ child has appeared
out of his meditations, and it stands,
cradled in his arms, upon the page.

All up and down the vestments of the saint,
paper money has been pinned, and in
the foreground on the left, a deacon stands
in waist-length stole, with salver at the ready,
who's grinning at the living child perched in
his father's arms in foreground opposite,
an envelope beneath his feet; he's been
handed a dollar, coached to make the offering.
I was this child, a greenback in my grip,
already practicing my lifelong habit:
to examine closely everything the world
puts in my hands, before I let it go.

I hold it, not done looking at the money.
My father, tilting out of frame, has realized
I'm not about to part with it. He turns
face to the camera, laughing. I look down.
The deacon, patient, grins. The marching band
my mother's cousins play in, snares and cornets

cracking in the summer air, vibratos
thick as meat sauce, brays and wobbles down
the street right by our house, as the procession
starts on its way again. This moment surely
doesn't last; the dollar, duly given up,
will find its way onto the vestments of
the saint, the patron of all that is lost.

I hold this photo in my hand today
and question it. I feel some mystery's
encoded in the composition – I
so like the child protected by the saint,
the page from which he sprang so like the money
drawn from the envelope between my feet.
But not until I read it differently
does it give up its secret, which lies not
in looking at the bill, but at my father:
he has a look I've never seen before.

My mother must have been behind the camera;
the glee my father shares is meant for her,
as they begin to learn what they have brought
into the world. Because I'm looking down,
distracted, he can show it – an expression
they both were careful not to let me see
thoughout their lives, though I could feel the pride
in their reserve. They always moderated
their response to a precocious child
whose curious interests must have mystified,
and whose early achievements got him noticed;
they didn't want me too full of myself.
Because I wasn't looking then, I can
see now what they kept between themselves.

~89~

To find a puzzle piece of the lost world
of childhood's rare; it's rarer still to find
the piece you didn't know enough to miss.
Standing above this case of memory,
I examine closely what is in my hand,
smile at my good fortune, then let go.

Not the Thing Itself

He was a widower, my mother said.
He lived a long time, didn't touch a thing
after his wife died, all her clothes still hanging
in their bedroom closet, in the dresser
drawers, he left things as they were. He met
my mother's high school friend a few years later.
They went out, eventually got married,
went on their honeymoon, with everything
still left untouched at home. She'd never seen
the bedroom. While they were away, it burned.
Not everything; the fire was selective.

The wife's half of the closet burned, her clothes
destroyed, his left undamaged. All the dresser
drawers were burned that held her things, not his.
Her half of the bed was charred, and in
their portrait the first wife neatly effaced;
smiling, his remained. Now this might sound
to you like a ghost story, but the second
wife, my mother's friend, thought otherwise.
She saw it as a blessing on her marriage,
the first wife bowing out dramatically.

I knew that couple. Old friends of my parents,
they used to visit with their daughter, who
was older than I was. Our folks would talk
and we'd play chess. You wouldn't think to sit
with them that something extraordinary
ever happened. They were regular,
it seemed to me, like anybody else.

My mother used to like to tell their story.
It's not the thing itself, it's how you take it.

1+1=One

The quiet rush as wind clears through the trees
is not the wind, is not the trees: alive
only as long as they're alone together.

One Saved From the Flame

*Conkers is a traditional children's game in Britain, Ireland, and
the US played using the seeds of horse chestnut trees. Two players,
each with a conker threaded onto a piece of string, take turns
striking each other's conker until one cracks.*

Freshly broken from its spiny capsule,
ruddy whorls of russet brown and auburn
spill across its shell like fingerprints
or storm fronts dipping down onto the prairie
seen from space. I dry the dampened surface
until it gleams and warms, then shudders from
the rubbing. Not for this the ice pick's tip
tuned in the blue gas flame, the piercing firm
and slowed to sear the chestnut's heart; no knotted
shoelace will suspend it, readied for
the blow, or hold it as it's spun and snapped,
the better for the cracking. Warm and glossy
from a thumb's caress, this Venus of
my eye will stay safe, pocketed away.

Other Waters

"You cannot step twice into the same river,
for other waters are continually flowing in."
— Heraclitus

If we could hear what Haydn heard
we'd hear it differently,
for Haydn hadn't heard a note
from recent centuries.

His tones evoked a world that he
was privileged to see;
but we have heard the chimes at midnights
darker far than he.

Chaos in his *Creation* seems
mere consonance to ears
benumbed at clashing intervals
repeated over years.

As we have lived through ages of
advanced anxiety,
so music's given voice to
faithlessness and cruelty.

Yet Haydn smiles, spreading *L'Aurore*
over our benighting;
through Haydn's eyes, surprised, we find
how sunnier the lighting.

Living in this millenium
with all that it provokes,

how badly needed are the laughs
we get from Papa's jokes!

If we could step farther upstream
into past history,
and shed our memories, there might be
true authenticity.

But as it is we have to make
contemporary art
some closer flowing parallel
and current counterpart.

Gut strings or steel alone don't make
our efforts laudable:
it's only playing in his mood
makes Haydn audible.

Outliers

Outliers, inarticulate, abstract
till given body by imagination,
unfelt emotions have minds of their own
and study ways to thrive among us, seek
entry past bolts unsettled, doors ajar,
like air that slips between window and sill
of the palatial real, to live within.
Meaning no harm, they need us as their hosts,
like heedless ants that creep across our floors.
Knowing how they overstay, we must
take care not to invite unwelcome guests:

Self-pity, like a dark-edged, spreading stain
invades the terraced borders of our sight
and tints us at the center till at last
our view's reduced to shades of monochrome.

Envy, immediate, outquicks and shouts
down our quiet, gentle joy in others'
just deserts – its whining appetites
a pet demanding shrilly to be fed
before all others, never satisfied.

Rubbed raw, the nerves reserved for feeling love
rebel: they send no further messages.
Diverted by their silence, pain pools up
and finds another route as we recoil
and mix the signals of a different heat.

The sweet taste of attention takes us by
surprise, melts on the tongue, increases height

~96~

by standing on its own shoulders, but can't
reach to the rim; the hole it's sinking in
is ever deeper incrementally.

Persuaded we're unworthy, we breathe in
the whiff of failure, deeply etherized
by the belief that bad things happen to us
for a reason: we deserve the worst.
The proof is that we get what we deserve.

Be careful what you think of. Better to
cajole the mind away than let it drift
into the fens where these contagions lurk.
We arm our devils when we think them tame.

Patching a Flat

for Everett Sprague

We had a lot of laughs together, Ev
and I. Our friendship thrived because we found
the same things funny – *almost* all the time.

"Okay," he said one day, "I got a joke.
This Japanese guy goes to see his doctor,
says 'I no see so good. You make this fast –
I double park my car' – The doctor looks
him over and says 'You got cataract.'
'No,' the guy says, 'Rincoln Continental!'"

I shook my head. "That's pitiful," I said.
"Demeaning, just for starters, and you're no
Buddy Hackett with the pidgin; it's not funny.
It's *almost* hopeless, but I'll tell you what –
I bet you I can make it funnier."

"Oh yeah?" Ev says, "I'd like to see you try it."

"Two wives are having lunch." I said, "One says
'My husband thinks he's funny, but he's not.
Just yesterday he told an awful joke
I didn't laugh at, so he got upset.'

'Men,' her friend says, 'I know what you mean.'

'I'll prove it,' says the first wife. 'let me try
it out on you. A man goes to his doctor,

a Japanese eye doctor, and says. "I
no see so good." The doctor looks him over,
and says to the man "You got cataract?"
So he says "no" – what's funny about that?"'

Piu Forte

My Nana Basile, born Maria Forte,
was just as strong by nature as by name.
Tall for her time, erect and spare, she lived
up to her nickname of Sunflower as
a girl, but grew to be a pillar to
her family of six. Her life got harder
in merciless old age, and she fought back
with unimaginable force, first as
a widow in her seventies, a brick
hot from the oven, wrapped in fresh newspaper,
placed at her feet to warm the empty bed.

A badly broken hip at eighty left
her stranded in a white hospital bed
compared to which Heine's *Matratzengruft*
was rosy-petalled. She was not to leave
it once over the sixteen years that followed,
though change came with a stroke at eighty-five.

She'd stare up at me when we visited,
and call me first my older cousin's name,
and then my father's, never mine, and reach
up to pinch my cheek, her good right hand
gripping me as she did life itself,
lopsided grin across her ruined face
lit up by those eyes that never flinched,
and grumbled "facce brutta!" pinning me
in place, and somehow squeezing even harder.

Now nearing seventy myself, as I
inspect my body for the early signs

of which part will betray me at the end,
I hope I have inherited the gene
that confers such stark tenacity.

Punch Drunk

During a long day's tracking, near to quitting,
familiar demons slip into the room
around the microphone, my horn, and me.

I play a chorus, and the engineer
says "two notes in that middle phrase weren't up
to pitch. I'll get you in two bars before it."

My solo picks up in the cans. Two bars
and I'm punched in to play the phrase again.
I do. We listen back. The same two notes
are out. We cue it up again. I blow the phrase,
lip up the vagrant notes. We listen back.

No dice. After a few more futile passes
I sense I'm too tired out, so I suggest
I just make up a different phrase to fill
the gap. We roll it back; I play another
phrase. I like it and it fits, but now
it seems a later note's a little out –
that is, the engineer hears it as flat
but I can't, so we listen back again.

We've reached the stage where we're not sure of sharp
or flat, but still can tell that something's wrong.
It's a good sign to knock off for the day,
but I say "Let me take just one more shot."

This time I don't come in at all. I pause,
say "Same place again." I hear my solo;
again I don't come in, because I can't

tell where I am. It seems my solo jumps
ahead all of a sudden, past the note
that cues me to begin. Either my mind
is giving way, or the recording app
is dropping out. The engineer assures me
that's impossible. He must be right.

The demons are in play. I know by now
not to try to fight them, so although
it means I've lost my mind I make no protest;
I simply ask to hear my solo from
the top, and that I be punched in whenever
he needs to do it. I repeat the lines
from the beginning, and that breaks the spell.

Later on I realize: my mind
was skipping back to the old punching cue,
except those notes I'd blown before had vanished
from the track when I changed up my solo.

We can erase the present and replace it,
but memory reminds us that the past
is in us still, insisting it exists.

Rainstick

Believed to have been invented in Chile or Peru,
but possibly traceable to older African origins, the
rainstick was used in ceremonies to evoke the rain spirits.

Sun-parched cactus branch shorn of its thorns,
their points turned inward, hammered through the wounds
into the hollow core, spines spiraling
in step-wise cascades, capped at either end,
dry pebbles heaped to bump and sift within,
its nutshell spaces ape the overcast
as air and gray mist rush up into showers.

The tilted stick whispers its sibilance.

Roy's Unlearned Lesson

Roy Eldridge Quartet, Sandy's – Beverly, Mass 1978

After his set, in which a European
trumpet player, younger and more "modern"
has sat in, Roy comes over to my table
in the dark part of the bar, and plunks
down next to me, and shakes his head.

"See, I just did a stupid thing," he says,
the high, bright edge of crackle in his voice,
if it could be seen, continuous
heat lightning in a muggy Southern night.
"I tried to beat him at *his* thing, instead
of playing *my* thing. I know better than that!"

His tone's exactly what he would have used
on me if I had made the same mistake:
dismay and exhortation mixed, to find
at sixty-seven, after fifty years
of taking each encounter as a joust
with everything at stake – you get no pass;
you have to learn again the unlearned lesson.

Secret Bird

for A.E. Stallings

Black bird comes from that far off place
where the moon's afraid to show her face
and secrets sleep in the holes in the ground
that their diggers believe will never be found.

But trees grow up from the sleeping seeds
and their branches bear the digger's deeds.
Black bird hops down from branch to branch
studies the trees in a careful dance.

The shiver of Spring, the blush of Fall
at last Black bird understands them all.
– Takes wing at a midnight's striking
flies to an ear he finds to his liking.

– Black bird wings through the dark
that keeps his mission hidden.
– Black bird chooses his mark
and comes to you unbidden.

Settles down close by your ear
silently as you're sleeping.
Doesn't give you a chance to fear
the secrets that's he's keeping.

Hops up close and bows his head
heavy with all he's found.
While you sleep the sleep of the dead
Black bird utters not one sound.

Sense and Sound

Not words alone, though sound is easiest
to share out in the open; private sense
instead: the slip of breath across the tongue,
the shape of air as tip dots letters at
the palate; all nerve endings tell the tale
of how the body feels words in the making.

As though I spoke and thrumming tissue pealed
like several bells in concert at the bone:
Keats' St. Agnes' Eve, "with lucent syrups,
tinct with cinnamon," and Rilke's "dunklem
Wein und Tausend Rosen," rolled up with
Hopkins' "ooze of oil crushed" and "with Ah!
Bright wings" combine to harmonize the thrill –

No closer can I come to duplicate
the sense of searching with my fingertips
your warm and pliant skin where curve of hip
encounters small of back and falls away,
its surface plush and yielding, yet beneath
firm to the core. Breath in my body as
I say these words feels closest to your touch.

Sensible Doubt

On radio we hear the residue
and instantly reconstitute a world
that might have left it, though the mind's eye lies
in taking coconuts for horses' hooves
and showing us a posse. We believe
in our imagination, though we know
it's possible that we deceive ourselves.

In ease of eyesight we are more naïve,
assuming light must show us everything,
so even when the young girl, upside down,
is seen to be a crone, we still believe
our eyes, as though we don't impose on both
a private version of reality.

We need another sense to realize
what leaves the visible as evidence.
But even if some deeper wave revealed
that all we can perceive is shadow to
some greater substance, in such other light
we'd struggle to conceive it, since the mind
constructs by memory as much as insight,
and if we ever knew a higher plane
we've all long since become amnesiac.

Unless perception brings us to that point
from which the shadows that comprise us fall;
until that light denied us lets us see
the place where they converge, still doubt your eyes.
Consider: sure as insight ends in umbra,
who knows the shadow knows the shadows lie.

Seven Hundredths of an Ounce

Newport, RI 1979

At the counter of *The Chocolate Soldier*,
surrounded by stupendous glassed-in sweets,
in that summer I turned thirty-one
and meeting you had summoned up a rare
affection I had never known before
and, so far, was not to know again,
in the quiet of the afternoon we splurged
on Belgian chocolate truffles, hazelnut
and tiramisu, cashew turtles, almond
bark the color of piano keys.

And on a whim I placed my finger down
on the electric scale, to see how light
my touch could be. Three times the numbers fell,
then I could do no less. At seven hundredths
of an ounce you softly cooed, delighted.

We had a future all that season; then
your past caught up, and we were overtaken.
I hadn't noticed: every time I took
my touch away, the scale went back to zero.

Sgt. Darden

Fort Leonard Wood, September 1970

Sergeant Darden marched us to the range,
fatigues starched blade-sharp even in the heat
of a Missouri summer, shades correct,
brim of his DI hat gently grinning.

No grin in Sergeant Darden as he taught us
how to aim and fire our M-16s,
most of us getting on a westbound plane
in five more months, him trying to get us ready
who wouldn't ever, couldn't ever be:
try as he might, some of our names were still
going to end up on a monument.
He did the best job that we let him do,
and took ten spoons of sugar in his coffee.

"Put your nose right up against the charging
lever, make that rear sight big. You'll see –
Expert," he barked, exhorting us, "don't mind
no kick, you be all right."
                                    I sprawled face down
and stuck my nose up tight against the metal,
the rear sight close as it could get, big as
a clock face, the front pin like matching hands
that pointed to six-thirty. It seemed like
I couldn't miss that way, although my nose
got red and powder lingered in my nostrils.

Weeks later, most of us days from the jungle,
we saw him for the last time, his smooth face

~110~

expressionless. He wished us luck, then fell
us out, and headed off toward next week's crop
of troops. But he walked by me close enough
that I could smell the congolene above
the heat, and said, resigned and quiet, "Son,
you were the only one that paid attention."

Song Unsung

for A.M.H

The singer, too long silent, holds his tongue.
Within, what's been withheld builds, past beginning,
so now, if once begun, it would exhaust
his listener; and so as not to be
too much, it must remain unheard, beneath
its heap of lost time, ever deepening.

Stazione Termini, Rome 1972

Unlike the well-kept train that brought me here
from Milan south to Rome, its passengers
fastidious and business-like, used to
the trip, attending to their own affairs,
conversing quietly, dozing, or reading,
this eastbound car headed to the Abruzzi
is loud with folk returning to their mountain
towns after a trip into the big city
for some necessities. Men, goats, and women
clog the aisle with bustle and outcry
until the train bumps into motion; then
they rush the windows, kneel to throw them open,
and showing soles of freshly store-bought shoes
they fill the row of windows to the shoulders.

I put my head out too, to see what they
are seeing: one long line of heads kerchiefed,
flat capped, or bare, all stretching to take in
the tableaux of the terminal as it
dwindles into the distance. I look down
now, where no one else is looking: brown
and black against the oily railbed lie,
in layers, thrown out heaps of used up shoes.

Stone Love

Don't give me any worthless paper love
not based on anything of value, that
you use to cover up your windows so
you can't see out, or start waste basket fires
that last about a minute. All those zeroes
on the back, and still a bushel full
won't buy a measly ounce of tenderness.

Look, I don't want to take you home, or follow
and spend the night in any place that scrip's
accepted. Where I come from love is stone.
I have to quarry it up in the mountains
where there's plenty, haul and roll a block
down through the passageways. It takes a lot
of time to push it to your door, but there
it's going to stay; big in your sight each morning,
still there for you, even if you move.

Straight Outta Antiquity

for Salvatore Raiti, 1895-1971

With one five foot length of line, designed
for hanging clothes, he made the ancient weapon.
Four knots, an S-curve, and a finger loop
were all he used. He took me to a field,
found some egg-sized stones, and showed me how
to cradle one, then set it spinning out
at arm's length overhead until the whir
pitched up; then the wrist snap and the letting
go, the stone straight, true to my intentions.

A shepherd boy in Sicily, he kept
the wolves at distance. Over here he cut
out leather soles and cobbled on the last,
illiterate till forty, learning then
Italian, never English. Proud to read,
he savored every word in the Italian
paper when it came each week. Through him
my line comes straight out of antiquity,
but up until him all unread, unwritten.

He launched me far into this field of letters.
Not here by accident, I'll use my sling:
spin out a taut line, singing in the air,
snap off a point, bound right between your ears.

Tempo Rubato

I drive today east of the Agawam,
straight through the light instead of turning left.
It's just as quick a way of getting home,
but it's an alternate I've been denied
nearly a year now while construction crews
replaced a faulty bridge over a stream.
The route is smooth again; its black top, fresh,
affords a layer of new memory.

I pass the western-lying fence and glance,
as I have done and written of before,
beyond the slatted apertures; the wood
again presents no obstacle. I see
the pool, the diving board, deserted in
November, and again the photo that
you sent me, taken fifty years ago
right here, of you, a standing cherub two
dripping steps away from water, brow
uncreased by care. These images, one made
by trick of vision in the outside world,
and one projected on my inner screen,
link up, superimposing as I glide
away. A team of workers took a year
to make this possible, and we both played
a part – coincidence, without a doubt,
no more. Intention didn't enter in,
yet calibration had to be exact
for me to realize the pieces fit.
Time steals on from itself; place lies in wait.

~116~

The Coventry Carol

Driving on the Solstice, tuning in
to Public Radio, I heard a voice,
legitimately trained, a little thin,
but earnest; the soprano's every choice

Sound, in phrasing and interpretation.
She made me think of High Church, vestments, chimes,
and incense wisping at a congregation –
a proper lullaby for modern times.

Once home, I craved the Voice Squad's plainer tones:
saw the shadows walk as blank light dimmed,
felt the dank chill in December's bones,
and tasted pewter on the tankard rim.

The Cracked Plate

I saw the crack while cleaning up the dishes
after lunch. The clear rinse water scudded
off the surface of the brindled plate
you bought us years ago, the only one
that's left from our long time together. Then
we used it rarely, saving it for special
occasions, but I like to use it now
for everyday. The water drained away
and there it was, straight as an interstate
and pointing up to midnight. So I thought
of you then, living down in Florida,
and married well if pictures tell the story,
by now some kind of graceful older lady.

"I'll always love you," you once said, "but I
won't always feel it." Time has proved you right.
What I feel is wrapped up mostly in
the way that neither of us had a child
after the one we would have had together.

We learn about good first, and better later,
and better still always appears to be
a possibility. We often see
the best in retrospect, after it's gone.

This plate's days are numbered. I could put
it in the cupboard, baby it with care,
protect what's left. Instead, I'll treat it like
it's still undamaged, use it every day.

~118~

The Ghost of Easters Past

March 31, 2013

The table is the same, my parents' plates
and silverware as well, brought from their house
after they died. The empty dinner chairs
surround me on three sides. Set out before
me, made by my own hands, this Easter dinner:
a rib roast, mushroom caps in gravy, green
glistening asparagus beneath
a scattering of slivered almonds, browned
potatoes with their darkened edges, all
delicious from the surety of skill
developed in the careful years I've lived
alone. A German Chocolate cake I've baked
awaits, its coconut and pecan frosting
ready to dress the single piece I'll serve
myself tonight, the rest piece by piece later.

I play for the occasion a recording
I made in secret at our Easter dinner
in Seventy-Nine; the family was large
then, boisterous, intact. The extra leaves
were added to my parents' dinner table,
and all the relatives had come to share
the afternoon procession of the feast
my Mother hurled for proof of love and power.

Knowing, as they did not, of the recorder
hidden beneath the window seat, I spoke
hardly at all throughout, and hours passed
as human chamber music, intimate,
dramatic, unimagined by Beethoven

or Janáček, was scrawled across the wall
of the holiday – all caught by the machine.

Now from home theater speakers in the basement
the distant voices of that day rise up;
the twisting open stairwell lets them reach
me, the floor ensures a separation.
All the characters joined in the riot
of parts below have passed away. A form
of resurrection lets them speak again
from memory, and only I remain
to listen to, and to extend, our story.

The Gradegrubbers

I love to see them writhe and squirm,
and plead their puny case.
I love the look of abject fear
that creeps upon each face.

And once I've let their spirits rise,
it almost makes me shout,
to see that little spark of hope
first flicker – then go out.

The Horn and Me

Rim width, bore and backbore, depth of cup
and cup configuration – the machinist
tools to the specifics where the metal
meets the lips. For the directed breath,
the mouthpiece is both barrier and entrance.

I set the embouchure, the muscles of
the facial ring fall into place around
the polished rim, the pressure of the lips
enough to keep the seal, but still relaxed
between the tensed up corners of the mouth.

I breathe in from the diaphragm, the broad
trunk muscles flex in concert as I lean
over my solar plexus. Then the air,
swift and pure in focus, concentrated,
up from my lungs, sets both my lips abuzz,
pours down into the mouthpiece opening.

The horn responds; it vibrates into voice
and I begin the daily litany:
long tones, lip slurs, scales, arpeggios,
up and down across the octaves. Once
begun, I may not take the mouthpiece from
my lips until it's done. Some days the horn
agrees, allows me sound without a challenge.
The notes unfurl like crisp flags in a breeze.

On other days the venture drifts awry
beginning with some small impediment:
a slight change in position of the lips,

some undigested morsel in my system,
my picking up the breath too far above
bedrock position – any, all contrive
to tick the airstream off its axis.

                             Then
the struggle to relax and strive at once
begins. The tones lunge into imprecision,
and moving up the scale becomes a gauntlet
of thinned out, bulged, or cracked and raspy notes –
or, when the horn balks at the push, air-stopped
silence. Tempted to rebel, the will
must gentle down, and patience settle in
throughout my body, led along a path
by hard-won increments up to completion.

But easy day or not, the horn abides.
Its large bore pipes, kept whistle-clean and open,
demand from me exactly what they did
decades ago. I am the variable.
The cornet holds the mirror up to me.
My nature is revealed, precisely what I bring
to each encounter. Unconcerned that I
succeed or fail, the horn exacts its due
and renders judgment audible. It lines
my body up behind my breath: corrects me.

The Man Who Couldn't Afford
to Buy a Vowel

with a nod to Ernest Vincent Wright

Here's to the man who can't afford a vowel:
His story's short or tall, but not a tale.
It never can begin, or ever end,
for he can start and stop, but not continue.
He can't imagine or remember it;
in fact he has no memory at all.

Though he can nap, he never sleeps at night.
His days have mornings but no afternoons.
He can brush his hair but not his teeth.
Sandals are fine, but never shoes or slippers;
socks are optional. He can have lunch
but not breakfast or dinner; no dessert.

He can't be on time, late, or even early.
Though Spring and Fall enchant him, he's confused
and doesn't recognize Winter or Summer.
Though he can walk and run, he doesn't dance.
He can read a book, but not the papers.
He can know it all, yet not be wise.

Compassion's in him without empathy.
He can be kind but never generous.
He can have a string of girls, but not
a wife; though he can feel infatuation
he never loves, or even likes, another.
To miss so much from such a small omission!

~124~

The Passing of the Age of Giants

March 28, 2015

"Where are the snows of yesteryear?" – Francois Villon

They hurry down, these modest flecks of wet
and whiteness, wind-directed to meander,
then settle, soaked up instantly at touch
of earth, already brimming with the winter melt.

Some greet the grainy surface of the crusts
remaining from the season past, to nestle
with them for a moment only, distant
relatives discovering each other
before a parting merciless and final.

Gale-driven snowfall and unbroken cold
had locked the landscape underneath a mask
that thickened with each application; gusts
had tarted up the drifts to an extreme.
The depths erased the outlines on the ground
and memory of other years alike.
No slackening: each week increased the grip
with fresh attention. Nothing softened; not
a trickle from the tree-thick ice stalactites
that poured from roofs and disappeared below
into the man-high whiteness.

                                    Through two weeks
ago, this winter's reign had held. But then
it was deposed, and a slow thaw set in
that's left us mired in wet, a few misshapen
islands of old white scattered about.

Now flakes laze slower, tentative and mild.
They are as temporary as can be,
these crystals barely making it to earth.
They'll blur no roofline, paint no branch today.
If some dirt-pitted patch, surviving from
those months of iron rule, offers the proof
of snow that bowed the earth under its yoke,
they're ignorant of common origin –
last only to be touched, then disappear.

The Poisoned Pawn

She was, it seemed, alone and unprotected,
hoping to be lifted from the board
and swept off to a place of safety on
the sidelines, set far from the clash of play.
She appealed to you, her would-be knight,
uniquely gifted as deliverer:
to save her was your common destiny.

Drunk on your secret wish to be a hero
you reeled into the action, heedless of
the unseen forces underfoot, until
the ground fell off beneath, and you were left
the one in need of saving, powerless
to make a move, knowing the game had changed,
feeling another's hand had made advances,
another's mind had planned the line of play.

This is your test: to see it is your grip
alone that holds you. Players must agree
to keep the game alive, so get up from
the board and walk away. Where rescue is
illusion, heroes lose themselves in action.

The Prisoner's Confession to the Jailer

From chains that others bound me in
I struggled to be free;
for no one had the right to limit
all that I could be.

But when at last the links were snapped
the door stood open wide.
I made no move to leave; instead
stayed quietly inside.

For other chains, invisible,
had power over me,
though he who tightened them was not
about to let me see.

All unaware I kept myself
where I fancied I belonged,
held by misapprehension;
nor could I guess how strong.

For it was I who had withheld
permission to be free;
preferring the familiar cell,
forbidding liberty.

In this blank state of ignorance
for years I stayed alone,
and might have been there still, had not
I wearied of the known.

One day my curiosity
outshouted expectation;
and though I felt it futile
I was moved to motivation.

We have our limitations,
I'd known that all along.
But could it be accepting them
might possibly be wrong?

I tried to stand, I tried to walk,
I brought myself to dare;
I found some doors were open
that I hadn't known were there.

I left that narrow prison cell,
and all those chains behind;
I traveled even faster
when I dropped them from my mind.

So hear this admonition
that I've carried from afar:
don't accept your limitations
before you learn what they are.

The Tree of Secrets

Because they crowded up within, I went
out at a moonless midnight, big with secrets
into the orchard. There, beyond a line
of pear trees, I fell on my hands and knees
and made a hole beside the clawed up earth
and bent down close, and whispered – all of it:

The hurtful truth which curdles on the tongue;
what shames by claiming we've a right to judge;
what utterance diminishes the speaker
revealing need when faced with greater need.
Whatever, once it's said, makes matters worse.

I whispered all of it, and filled the hole
back up to level, so there was no mark
of what I'd done, and walked away unburdened.

And overnight a tree grew on the spot,
all bare black branches stretched against the sky
like hands that beg no further questioning.
As seasons passed it bore no fruit, presented
not a leaf or speck of color. When
the cold returned, night birds assembled there
and roosted, brooding silently, a presence
which at a sign will rise as one, and wheeling
to seek you out, unerringly, will settle
all around you as you sleep. Then one
with iridescent wings will hop up close,
its dark head sleek and shiny by your ear
and bend to you and whisper – what? No tell-
tale creature, he will utter not a sound.

The Winnowing

Father's Day, 2016

They came as animals, like deer appearing
at the fringe of trees behind my house,
I lying under bright sun in the silence
of the heavy afternoon. They glided
one by one across the grass and dipped
their heads to drink from the white plaster basin
of the chipped birdbath, brimming still from last
night's shower. Then they looked at me, their eyes
widened, quiet, glistening, as though
they had to get accustomed to the light
as I would to the sudden darkness of
the house if I stepped in there for a moment.

The first approached, a fawn, with budding antlers,
velvet nubs, just broken through above
its brow. Gentle and unafraid it drew
near to where I lay, and seemed to speak:

"I am the boy who is to be your first
born. Though both too young, you love my mother
well, and you will choose to sacrifice
the future you expect, out of a sense
of duty. Without knowing it at first
you'll hold that against her, and finally me.
And I will feel that. You will stay together;
your unhappiness will grow with me,
and I will blame myself beyond all reason,
working hard to please, to make things right.

When I take my life at seventeen,
feeling powerless, my means will be
undemonstrative, and you won't see
it coming. Nor will my apology,
left in a careful note, make sense to you.
No one else will understand your pain,
and you will stay together even after
that, unable to live past the sharing."

Sad-eyed, he moved away. As though I held
out some threat, a spotted stag approached,
with eyes more wary, antlers razor-pointed
branching wide, bolder of seeming voice:

"You'll meet my mother on a trip. Both far
from home in a bewildering city, not
knowing the language of that place, you'll find
a haven in each other's voice. Brief lovers,
you'll return to different countries. When
my mother writes to tell you, there'll be no
thought you'll be together. When she says
she means to raise me by herself, without
demand, reproach, or even expectation,
your protest is at best half-hearted, and
short lived. You go on with the life you've planned.

Until my mother dies I never know you.
I'll seek you out then, thinking you untroubled,
my heart set against you even though
she always held you blameless. Envious
but needing your acceptance, I'll appear
and find you open but disabled by
unreasonable guilt. Caught in that current

we'll circle then, helpless and endlessly
trying to approach, yet keeping distance."

Tilting his head, he slanted off, but stayed
nearby as a third approached, a doe
that bobbed her head and nuzzled at my hand.

"I am your youngest child," I seemed to hear,
held by her quiet eyes. "My mother will
be only twenty when you meet, and yet
she'll seem to understand you, and accept
what you will become. Her love will reach
a part of you you thought unreachable,
and joy will have a freshly minted meaning.

But joy in common use soon wears its features
down, and it becomes dumb to the touch.
Her feelings all will dull, and she will be
beyond your power to console, despondent,
sinking where you cannot follow, or
choose to follow if you could. And every
moment she compares her state to yours
she'll slip down deeper, dropping out of reach.
And out of her despair I will be born,
bearing the inexplicable: the gift
to grow, against the odds of my surroundings,
untouched by trouble, generous and loving,
patient with the limits of my strength.

I'll understand her distance, and return
a warmth that somehow will not drive her down.
I'll give her what she can't accept from you,
and ease the burden of your broken love.
I'll apply that grace throughout her life,

and be a balm to you when she is gone,
healing those places rubbed raw by a life
in harness to a sledge that couldn't move.
You'll feel that I'm the best thing in your life."

She lifted up her head and drifted off,
still gazing at me, as it seemed, intently.
The three of them, in a deliberate way,
stepped carefully across the grass, toward
the line of trees. After a subtle swishing
of crushed pine needles made its mark upon
the silence of the afternoon, the darkness
of the trees beyond concealed and closed
them up, leaving the yard, it seemed, untouched.

I lay there, thinking how they saw their futures
as clearly as I did my past. And yet,
in my own life not one of them had lived.
Their mothers never bore them. They went on
to different lives beyond our time together,
with marriages to others, but no children.
I'd somehow blamed myself for that, and been
blamed in return, though we'd agreed each time
that it was better not to let them live.
Better perhaps. There still seemed little good
could come of it. Each time we'd split apart
not long after, as the faith we had
about the future shrivelled up and fell
away. What would have been had always stayed
a question. Now these creatures came, after
a lifetime on my path, with neither blessing
nor rebuke, as though they'd lived their story,
and those three women whom I'd loved and I
were the only ones deprived of it.

Our choices had no power over them,
their lives already written, undisturbed
before their birth; only our own could change.

That winnowing has left me in my life
by my own choice last of my line, alone.
I rose as clouds came drifting from the West
to interrupt the rush of summer light,
and went into the house to fix my dinner.

To My Brother the Dancer

for Billy Siegenfeld

Like you my body is my instrument.
Like you what springs up in me first is rhythm;
down the spine it goes, crackling its way
inside the knees, between the vertebrae.
Back in the brain the urge is: yes, to move.

Tonesmith

Like any other score, these words are merely
shadows on the page, a rough instruction
to the reader, two dimensional:
until you hear me speak them, incomplete.

It takes the playing to release their music.
Overheard from an adjoining room and through
a wall that shears them of their meaning, leaving
clack and slip of consonants, the knock
of rhythm, ribbon bend of melody
from forte down to pianissimo,
they still deliver essence on their own.

Heard face to face, they add what else a word
can do in company: tell you a story,
paint a picture, raise the dead, and tell
that truth that makes you laugh or starts you thinking.
You'll get that from the page. But hear me play
these compositions on my instrument.

Two Simple Verses on the Way Things Are

At Present:

Don't know how the frog got in the well.
He ain't sure himself how he got there.
Can't jump high enough to break the spell,
but he don't know it, and the well don't care.

Afterward:

Don't know how he got out of that well.
Frog ain't sure himself how he got free.
Did someone help him out? That's hard to tell –
looks now like it was always meant to be.

Waiting for Ellington

The Grist Mill, Seekonk, Mass 1972

Between the band bus and the club's back door
we waited in a line. We'd read he always
traveled by car, with Harry Carney driving.
They'd have to walk right by us, young musicians,
throwback swingers, each in awe of Duke,
thinking the same thing. Our drummer John
was saying it out loud. "What does a guy
like me have to say to Ellington?
What's *he* got to hear from *me*?" We stood
our ground, affecting nonchalance we thought
that Duke might value, shifting weight from one
foot to the other. Then the car pulled up,
and Harry Carney got out. Finally
Duke himself emerged and swept our way,
his No-Loose-Buttons, Not-Brown overcoat
as dap as next year's fashion. What we hoped
would be At Ease was Full Attention as
he drew up to us, showing no expression.
We stood stock still, forgot to take a breath.
When he got face to face with John he paused.
"Say," he grinned, "don't I *know* you from someplace?"

Waldszenen

New Year's Day, 2015

*"The distinction between past, present, and future
is only an illusion, however persistent."* — Einstein

Deep in the old year's final hour I sit,
my thoughts on friends who passed under the number.
Der Vogel als Prophet fills in the dark,
its forest palpable here in this room.

Dimmed by the mechanism used to save it,
the shade of Cortot takes the shape of Schumann.
Each note across the flitting figures given
its own tint, the bird is bodied out
in variegated tones, and tells of time
suspended. Shading in the mystery,
the sound is ancient and immediate.

The past is no more gone than we are; no
more here than we are. In three minutes at
the keyboard in the last mid-century,
Cortot walks in Schumann's forest from
a century before, and brings back proof:
the *meno mosso* central section speaks
in gliding tongues of what is yet to come
to all of us, within the mystery.

The fluttering resumes without a warning.
In a minute there is just the noise
of the machine. The clock hands stand straight up;
the year has turned while I have been away.

War Games, 1953

Father's Day, 2013

Before the bowl, the little boy directs
a stream down on the dozen floating butts
encountered in the bathroom. The flotilla
he imagines, blasted one by one
with pin-point aim, explodes its paper hulls
and leaves tobacco wreckage in its place.
Blind god of war, he lords it over them.

He sees it finally, after sixty years:
the cigarettes were Camels. So his Dad
had hidden every day and smoked upstairs.
Less than a decade then after the War,
he never spoke of the Pacific Theater,
his time in Fiji, or Guadalcanal.
Since his malaria attacks had stopped
some years after his marriage, he had led
what looked to be a normal life. What secrets
kept him pacing in a narrow room
alone, pitching a bowlful of spent butts
in flicked arc after arc into the water
through smoke and silence, far from sympathy?

Well-lit Corridors

I learned to crawl, then walk, playing the blues,
the goal to move with ease through all the keys.
The chords were darkened corridors at first;
I felt my way by steps, and found my footing
as similarity became familiar.

But standards were forbidding structures; strange
and unexpected chords surprised me with
their twists and funhouse turns, baffled my steps;
reaching the bridge of "Have You Met Miss Jones?"
I'd tilt the wrong way, stumbling in the dark.

I made every mistake I couldn't help
and played through, getting used to new directions.
Accustomed now, each standard is a chance
to move another way, the halls well lit
in time for me to saunter, skip, or dance.

Windows and Doors

"The sun illumines the night,
it does not turn it into light."
         — Antonio Porchia

After we'd known each other for a day,
I dropped you off at night at your hotel.
A morning flight would take you far enough
away for me to feel we'd never meet
again. We sat two minutes in the car,
spoke haltingly around unanswered questions,
and then you said goodbye and turned away.

I put my hand out, resting it a moment
on your back, along the twisting bones,
and felt a window open through the touch
that spilled a future like a sudden rush
of sun against my skin. I let that light
guide me to the promise of another
meeting, though I had to wait for years.

At second touch your body was a door.
I pored over each surface inch and seam
at close attention; opening, it led
into an unlit, airless, empty room.

Winter Light

Lulled by its lavish stores, my eyes have squandered
summer light. Now in December, tilting toward
the solstice, reveling in brevity
the morning light reveals the truth of cold
beyond my window. In the slender mid-day
the low sun speaks its piece and hurries home.
I see by glint of winter clarity.

ABOUT THE AUTHOR

Al Basile is a poet, singer/songwriter, and cornetist; he was the first recipient of a Master's degree in Creative Writing from Brown University in 1970. He began his career as a cornet player with Roomful of Blues in 1973, and has worked with the Duke Robillard Band since 1990. He has fourteen solo CDs under his own name, which regularly reach the top 15 on the *Living Blues* airplay charts. He has six Blues Music Award nominations as best horn player, and his 2016 release *Mid-Century Modern* was nominated as Best Contemporary Blues Album. He also spent 25 years as a private school teacher. His poetry and fiction have been published regularly since he left teaching in 2005. His first poetry collection, *A Lit House*, was published in 2012, and in 2015 he was co-winner of the Meringoff Award for poetry, given by the Association of Literary Scholars, Critics, and Writers.

The author's reading of the poems in this book
may be accessed at:
http://albasile.com/Tonesmith_-_audio_files.html

This book has been set in Garamond, a typeface created by Claude Garamond in the first part of the Sixteenth Century. He based his font on types cut by Francesco Griffo for Venetian printer Aldus Manutius in 1495. Garamond created a typeface with an unprecedented degree of balance and elegance, for centuries standing as the pinnacle of beauty and practicality in type-founding. Italics for the Garamond font are based on those cut by Robert Granjon (1513–1589).

To order additional copies of this book
or other Antrim House titles, contact the publisher at

Antrim House
21 Goodrich Rd., Simsbury, CT 06070
860.217.0023, AntrimHouse@comcast.net
or the house website (www.AntrimHouseBooks.com).

•

On the house website
in addition to information on books
you will find sample poems, upcoming events,
and a "seminar room" featuring supplemental biography,
notes, images, poems, reviews, and
writing suggestions.

www.ingramcontent.com/pod-product-compliance
Lightning Source LLC
Chambersburg PA
CBHW021439080526
44588CB00009B/597